# Why Play Anywhere Else?

## HOW WE BUILT STICKS BASEBALL INTO A NATIONAL BRAND

# CHASE BREWSTER

Ainsley & Allen Publishing

ISBN:    978-1-946694-64-5 (eBook)
         978-1-946694-65-2 (paperback)

To my dad, Dave Brewster.
Without you, there is no story to tell.

# Contents

# Foreword

You know, it's kind of poetic that as I am putting my thoughts together for this foreword, I'm on the road in Florida, dropping my son off at college. It's his freshman year, continuing his education – as well as his lifelong love of playing baseball. Poetic because I can connect a direct line from this moment back to the day I first met Chase Brewster, whose story I'm privileged to introduce.

My relationship with Chase goes back a few years to when I was starting a youth baseball program to prepare young players to compete at the high school level. At the time, I didn't know much about him, only that he was the coach for the Genoa Central High School team that would occasionally use our indoor practice facility. To be honest, I hadn't paid much attention to him until someone suggested that he might be a good candidate to oversee our high school program – that's when our paths truly converged.

I have to admit, my first impression of Chase was one of skepticism. I thought, "This is the guy we should turn the high school program over to?" At least in my mind, he didn't exactly look like the typical elite high school coach. But man, was I in for a surprise.

After talking to him for a few minutes and watching him work with the players, any doubts I had evaporated. Chase had this incredible knowledge of the game, and the way he communicated with the players was unlike anything I'd seen before. He and I have coached together for a long time, and his unique ability to inspire and connect with people is truly special. It's funny how one encounter can set the course for a lifetime of friendship and shared purpose.

Chase's drive and passion are something to behold. He just doesn't know how to quit. He would drive countless hours, sometimes as much as 18 hours straight, just to get to a tournament. Then, he spent the entire weekend, coaching, and mentoring these young players in non-stop games. And when it's all said and done, he hops right back on the road, thinking ahead to the next tournament.

Now, doing that for your own kids might seem like a given, but Chase? He does it for other people's kids. It's a level of dedication that's something else altogether. Tournament after tournament, he keeps at it. That's a grind, no doubt about it. It takes an immense amount of work and preparation, more than most people fully grasp.

Chase has this relentless drive to always improve, both as a coach and as a businessperson. He's constantly on a quest to learn how to get better at what he does. It's not just about staying in his comfort zone; he actively seeks out information from a wide variety of sources and is always on the lookout for new knowledge and insights.

We have regular conversations about it. But here's the thing about Chase – he's not just a sponge soaking up all this wisdom for himself. He's one of the most giving and unselfish individuals I've had the privilege of knowing. He's not trying to hide some secret sauce; he genuinely wants to share what he learns with others. It's this unique combination of a constant pursuit of knowledge and an open-hearted willingness to share that sets Chase apart.

Witnessing Chase's transformation first-hand over the years has been nothing short of remarkable. I got to watch a struggling coach evolve into a visionary leader who would take Sticks Baseball from just another summer team to an organization nationally recognized as a launch pad for aspiring athletes and a deep source of talent by college recruiters and pro scouts. A journey you're about to see up close in his book.

You'll quickly discover that Chase isn't just a coach; his expertise goes way beyond the baseball field. His approach to team management and player development, characterized by meticulous thought and preparation along with the stories he shares in these pages, provides some invaluable lessons.

But more than just a baseball story, this book is about the human spirit, dreaming big, embracing mentorship, and staying true to your principles. It's about the importance of community, the power of support networks, and overcoming life's challenges. Chase's journey is a roadmap for anyone looking to blaze their own trail and make a meaningful impact.

I didn't hesitate at the opportunity to write this foreword. It just felt like the right thing to do because Chase's story is one of resilience, belief, and transformation, and it deserves to be shared. It's a story about chasing dreams and putting in the hard work to make them come true.

Any team or business would be fortunate to have someone like Chase leading their organization. He's not just a coach; he's a mentor and a role model, which is why he has such a dedicated following and makes such a profound impact on people's lives, far beyond the baseball field. There are countless examples of kids who played for him, and even though their baseball days are behind them, they still want to be close to his program. That speaks volumes about the kind of person he is and the mark he leaves on people.

Chase Brewster is truly a remarkable individual, and I'm honored to call him a friend.

So, I invite you to dive into "Why Play Anywhere Else: How We Built Sticks Baseball into a National Brand" by Chase Brewster. It's not just a sports story; it's a testament to the power of determination and a reminder that with hard work and dedication, you can achieve your dreams and make a real difference in the lives of others.

Steve Landers Jr.

# Prologue

*"Your value is much higher than you
think to a small number of people"*
– Daniel Priestley

God has a way of being funny sometimes. My wife Alisha and I, along with the Slaytons, are heading to Hawaii for a family vacation. For months, I've been telling myself that I would finish this book on our almost ten-hour flight.

Our Delta One seats are equipped with every amenity I could ask for – a full bed, a complete entertainment system, lunch, dinner, and snacks. Ironically, one of the most important things is missing... Wi-Fi!

When the captain announced, "I apologize, but there will be no Wi-Fi on this flight," I knew it was God's way of telling me to get to work. Nothing says you can change the world like waking up from a three-hour nap in your own bed, thirty thousand feet above the ocean. This unconventional writing location has surprisingly become the easiest place for the words to just flow.

I've always had a complicated relationship with flying, marked by a mix of motivation and deep-seated fear. I would get night terrors before a flight and usually talk myself into driving instead. But over time, I've learned the key to overcoming this fear... just fly more. Luckily, my wife and I have careers that require us to travel quite a bit each year. Flying private has helped diminish my fear, but for this trip to Honolulu, it wasn't an option. Still, watching the pilot work and realizing I have no control over the situation somehow puts my mind at ease. I guess I'll make do with the six-foot bed of Delta One.

Looking out the window at God's creations from five miles above, I can't help but reflect on the incredible things He has done in my life. This flight, this moment, seems like the perfect time to share the foundations upon which we built our business and the journey from its inception to where it stands now.

If you are reading this, it means I finally achieved one of my lifelong goals – writing a book. Thirty-four years on earth and fifteen years in coaching have provided me with a wealth of experiences and lessons which I now feel it's time to put down into words. Initially, I thought I would write a biography, but this book turned out to be about business leadership, a direction I never expected.

What started as an idea for a biography about me has evolved into a narrative about making our business successful and my journey from working for free to turning Sticks into a national brand. This book is filled with never-before-told stories about my life, the company, and the path we took to get where we are today. While it's not strictly a baseball book, it's certainly a common theme framing the success Sticks has achieved and these ten pillars of success, I believe, are versatile enough to be applied in any business context.

As I continue to type away, I realize this book is more than just a collection of words. I think of it as a piece of art – at least in the sense that it will never be perfect or finished, but getting it to print was the goal, and here we are at the finish line.

This book is by far the biggest blessing of my career. It pushed me out of my comfort zone, demanding skills beyond my professional domain. The hardest part was starting – picking up the pen and writing the first word on January 22, 2023. It's a challenge because it opens me up to judgment in an area where I lack prior experience. But the importance of writing this book, the need to share what I've learned over a decade in business, is bigger than any fear. It's not about seeking fame on social media or the potential revenue from book sales; it's about fulfilling a dream and sharing insights that might help even just one person better their situation.

I owe so much to my incredible wife, family, mentors, and circle of friends. Without them, this story wouldn't exist. While I can't speak for the paths that other successful people have taken, I can share mine.

But first, I must say thank you! Thank you for supporting me and my dream. I'm not sure how this book will be received, but in my heart, it's already a five-star review. I've poured my heart and soul into this project. It was not only an extremely vulnerable endeavor, but also tough mentally.

I like to think I'm smart and educated, but putting thoughts into words and sentences with correct spelling and grammar is another level of education that I don't claim to have. I started writing this book on January 22, 2023, after years of saying I would. Two months of nonstop writing later, we began editing, only to find there was much more work to do. Organizing stories into the pillars of success and making sure they flowed smoothly took a lot of time and effort. But here we are!

# Introduction

# You Can Change the World

*"Think beyond your lifetime if you want to*
*accomplish something truly worthwhile"*
– Walt Disney

If you've got a dream you're chasing, the best advice I can give is to just start. It's never going to be perfect right away, but you won't get better, master your craft, or have a chance to move forward in your field until you start.

Before diving into the 10 pillars, let me share a bit of my backstory. Why would you take advice from someone you don't know?

My life's pretty much an everyday story. Mom was an addict, Dad worked 80 hours a week to keep the lights on for me and my brother, and somehow, I ended up being the first in my family to graduate from college. I got to be a student assistant for Coach Will Bolt at Texarkana College from 2007 to 2009, then an Assistant Coach in 2010. Coach Bolt's now the Head Baseball Coach at the University of Nebraska and being around him every day did something for me personally and professionally that I can't ever repay. Lance Harvell and Brad Flanders, who were also on our staff at Texarkana College, are doing great too – Harvell's with Coach Bolt at Nebraska, and Flanders is with the Philadelphia Phillies after his time at Abilene Christian University and the University of Arkansas.

2011 marked a significant shift for me—a change in scenery, state, and professional level. After winning two Conference Championships at Texarkana College, I found myself in Kelly Green, working with Jonathan Gosdin at Genoa Central High School in Texarkana, AR. What I thought would be a one-year, internship-like job turned into seven of the best years of my life, yielding five Regional Championships, four Conference Championships, and two State Championships. Eventually, my journey in Genoa Green came to an end.

At this point, you might think this is just another business book where someone brags about their achievements, and you could not care less. Ten years ago, you wouldn't have believed I'd have enough money or knowledge to fill these pages.

In 2013, I was at my happiest working at Genoa Central High School, making $17,000 a year. We were coming off our first State Championship, ranked number one in the state again, and I was with the love of my life for five years. How much is 17K a year? So little that I couldn't afford to ask Alisha to marry me. We were together for over ten years before I could propose, simply because I didn't make enough money. Alisha never pressured me to choose a different career or set a deadline for marriage, as you sometimes hear. I couldn't ask for a better life partner, and now she can get anything she wants after waiting so patiently.

If you're reading this book expecting a story of me going from one of the lowest paid in my profession to a millionaire in ten years, you'll be disappointed. The story is short: God blessed me immensely. I have no other way to explain it because I shouldn't be writing this book. Apart from His love and blessings, we treated everyone right and worked harder than everyone else. That's the truth. I have the best group of people around me, and we all move to the same beat. In this book, you'll find the ten pillars of success that have put me and our entire team in a position where I can't even imagine what the next ten years will look like.

In my seven years at Genoa Central, I served every role imaginable, including being the Head Coach in 2015. That year, we won the Regional Championship and had the most wins of any 3A team in Arkansas. My two years as Co-Head Coach with TJ Cox were pivotal, culminating our journey in an unforgettable way with another Regional Championship.

This brings us to my current profession. I am the Founder, Owner, and President of Sticks Baseball, which started in 2016 while I was still at Genoa Central. We provide a summer and fall baseball program for high school-age players, mainly between 15 and 18, to play when their high school teams are not in season. Our busiest months are late May through July, and September and October. We also have youth Sticks teams, ages 7 through 14, affiliated with us through partnerships with other facilities.

While our base is in Arkansas, we have had players from Texas, Louisiana, Kansas, Nevada, Minnesota, Florida, Missouri, South Carolina, Oklahoma, Connecticut, Hawaii, Arizona, New York, Georgia, California, and even internationally from places like the Dominican Republic and Canada. Notably, Pauly Santana, the number two MLB.com ranked International player and current Texas Ranger outfielder, played with us.

We grew Sticks from two teams to five, then ten, and eventually to twenty-five high school teams during COVID-19. This success led me to turn this hobby into a full-time job in the fall of 2017. Despite my initial fears, I am thankful for taking that leap of faith. Eight years later, we have built a nationally ranked program that plays in the biggest events and was recently named the Chicago White Sox Scout Team. Over these eight years, we've had over 550 players commit to college baseball, 53 MLB Draft Picks, and three players debut in the Major Leagues. As we move forward, I hope these numbers continue to rise. In this book, I'll share more about what makes Sticks so special, and how it operates both on and off the field.

Now that I've shared a bit about my family, career, and current business, I hope you're comfortable listening to advice from someone you've just met. Don't worry, there'll be more stories along the way, before you finish this book, you'll feel like we're old friends. Just know that my hope is for everything I share to help you and your business as much as it has helped me.

I've always been skeptical of motivational books and speakers. One of my best friends used to sit around watching one particular motivational guru's videos all day and send me his favorite clips. I couldn't help thinking this was just a guy "acting" for likes and views. I didn't know much about the guy but I quickly concluded that these videos weren't a true reflection of him but rather an actor doing their job.

In 2022, my New Year's resolution was to read 52 books. Books had become a huge part of my life, and I wanted to read more. I'd often find myself exploring different topics, jumping from one subject to another. After reading two books by the same author, I looked up whether he had any online interviews or podcasts, which of course he did. Having listened to hundreds of his podcasts, I realized that this audio form of learning had become my new "book." I was becoming obsessed with absorbing all I could from successful people, especially those outside of baseball. If you're curious about my favorite reads, below is a list of my top ten favorite books that I've read so far. This is a habit I adopted from Jesse Cole. Like him, I want to share as many positive publications as possible, hoping they impact you as they did me.

- *LeBron, Inc* – Brian Windhorst
- *Fans First* – Jesse Cole
- *Unreasonable Hospitality* – Will Guidara
- *The Power of Habit* – Charles Duhigg
- *Born to Shine* – Kendra Scott
- *Chase The Lion* – Mark Batterson
- *I Can't Make This Up* – Kevin Hart
- *Pour Your Heart into It* – Howard Schultz
- *Oversubscribed* – Daniel Priestley
- *Find Your Yellow Tux* – Jesse Cole

Each quote under the chapters comes straight from notes I took while reading—those bits that grabbed my attention and wouldn't let go.

What I've realized is that stories of highly successful people are inherently motivational. My issue wasn't with my friend's motivational guru or his message; my disconnect was due to not knowing his story, which prevented me from seeing the motivational aspect. Everyone experiences motivational messages and stories differently. After absorbing hundreds of podcasts and reading numerous books, I felt compelled to share my own motivational story and the strategies behind Sticks Baseball's success.

Many books have altered my perspective and life outlook. An analogy that particularly resonated with me was from Mark Batterson in "Double Blessing," which introduced the concept of "be an umbrella." This idea is something I think we can all incorporate into our lives. An umbrella doesn't stop the rain or adjust the forecast. It doesn't dispel the sunshine or keep the sleet and snow at bay. What it does do, however, is keep you safe and dry during a downpour, providing protection when you need it.

Years of fear about failing in writing this book have brought me to this moment that you're reading. This is not just a story about me, but about everyone who works for Sticks Baseball, and all that we did to build it into what it is today with no prior experience in this field. We grew Sticks Baseball from the ground up as a team, turning it into one of the top summer baseball programs in the country. Every logo, every design, every phone call, and every decision were a team effort. I owe it to everyone who has helped us along the way to publish this book.

No matter how often my wife tells me, "No one is going to read your book," I am excited to finally share our story with the world. The current title, "Why Play Anywhere Else: How We Built Sticks Baseball Into a National Brand," wasn't our original title when we began meeting with publishers. As I worked on this project, I kept thinking about the title "You Can Change the World," and how we could share the ten principles that built our business to help others in their endeavors.

I've always been a team player and taken pride in my team. In my mind, it was about "me and my team." But by the end of 2022, my focus shifted to helping others, especially those close to me. I've always wanted everyone around me to succeed, but I began feeling guilty about my success, especially when my closest friends and family weren't experiencing the same. It wasn't just about "me and my team" anymore; it was more about "how can I help my team." I was particularly troubled by my dad having to work hard into his sixties, while I was sleeping until 11 am every day. I realized that without his sacrifices, there would be no Sticks Baseball or the lifestyle I have.

After reading Steve Harvey's book "Act Like a Success, Think Like a Success," I started making my vision board. On August 25th, 2022, I wrote down goals that I still carry with me:

1.  Make ALT Magazine's "23 People to Watch in 2023"
2.  Attend church more in 2023 than in 2022
3.  Enable my dad to quit his job
4.  Get my best friend a full-time job with Sticks Softball
5.  Ensure Alisha can travel more in 2023

When I finished my vision board, I felt proud of where my focus was. Even though part of me wanted to make a magazine cover for a bit of vanity, the rest of my goals, the ones that would truly bring me joy, had nothing to do with me. I realized I needed to work harder to provide for my family and help those in my circle succeed. I would go on to make it to the cover of "23 People to Watch in '23."

Reading more books in 2022 was the thread that connected it all for me. Inspired by Jesse Cole's "Fans First," I got the idea to start writing handwritten letters to our latest group of players. I found myself frequently signing off with "Don't ever forget, you can change the world."

The more times I wrote that phrase, the more it cemented my belief in it. It evolved from a simple sign-off to the impactful final words a player would see before the note's closure, a perfect end before a new beginning. Something that would stick with them when self-doubt would creep in. Both for them, and for me.

I began to send texts and emails to our players, each one a reminder that I believed they could change the world. The more I said it, the more it felt like my responsibility to make sure they believed it too.

In January 2023, I wore the "You Can Change The World" Sticks hoodie which had become somewhat famous. People loved it. After we returned from Arizona, I made up my mind: all the gear for the players that summer would carry this message. I wanted every player, every coach, to see it, read it, memorize it, and most importantly, believe it. It was important enough that I decided to put it on our coaches' pullovers as well. At that point, there was no turning back.

The pillars of success I've outlined in the next ten chapters have not just worked for me; they've propelled me to the forefront of my field at 34. If my 24-year-old self had been able to read this book, it would have changed my life. Everyone's pillars of success will differ, and that's perfectly fine. What's important to me may seem trivial to you, and vice versa. There are no absolute right or wrongs when it comes to the foundations of success. Growth alters perspectives over time. I hope that in ten years, my pillars will have evolved, reflecting further growth and success.

Whether you are a coach, business owner, or both, my genuine hope is that you enjoy this book and find it beneficial in your daily life.

# Pillar #1

# Be Curious, Creative,
# and Selfish with Your Time

*"Be the star of your own movie"*
– Skip Bertman

For the better part of a decade, I feel like I outworked everyone in my profession. I didn't turn down an invitation to watch a single game or a request to coach an event, even if it meant taking a financial loss.

I figured out pretty quickly that social media had become a virtual resume for coaches and athletic directors to see in real-time. So, I would post every chance I got, just to make sure the players knew that I loved supporting them and to let everyone else know how hard I was working.

In those early years, I worked a lot of long hard hours for free or close to it, making a lot of sacrifices to live out my dream.

Regrets? None. I'd do it all over again in a heartbeat.

For years, my close friend Shaun Manning insisted that I needed to hire someone to manage the daily operations of Sticks Baseball. The idea seemed extravagant. Growing up in a family that didn't have a lot of money, the thought of paying someone just to field calls and emails seemed crazy to me. I clung to the mantra, "Never let anyone outwork you." But eventually, the relentless pace took its toll. I was worn out. Every call seemed to drag on for an interminable twenty minutes, only to end with a bigger pile of missed calls and notifications waiting for me.

One particularly grueling day, I tallied up all the calls in my log; by 6:00 pm, I counted 100, and that was because I hit the limit of what my phone displayed. The total was undoubtedly higher.

The turning point came in the summer of 2020. More than 400 high school players and 25 high school teams—the highest number in Sticks' history—signed up to play summer ball after missing out on their high school season, which was canceled due to COVID. Our partner programs in Arizona and New York were signing up even more players and teams from both coasts.

Although Texas and Arkansas were still closed from the pandemic, we were getting commitments from tournament directors in Georgia and Tennessee, states that were ahead of the curve, to start playing in late May. But parents expressed their doubts and were reluctant to make payments.

My call volume tripled with parents asking about our backup plans and refund policies. I was taking every call, answering every email, and working as the manager of every department. I felt like I was running the pharmacy, grocery, clothing, and appliance departments at Walmart - while doing oil changes on my lunch break. It was exhausting and was ruining my love for something that meant so much to me.

I spent every second doing something other than what I was great at—getting players recruited to play college baseball. There was just no time to talk to college coaches because my days were spent answering the same questions over and over. I knew something had to change.

Shaun Manning's advice started to sound not so crazy.

When you build something that means as much as the Sticks means to me, finding someone to step into your shoes, be in places you can't be, and make decisions with the same mindset can seem like an impossible task.

"There's was no way I can find someone who matches my way of thinking and my love for this organization," I thought. And even if there was such a person out there, I figured they would have likely started their own program by now.

I needed someone I could mold into the position. The right person doesn't have to know everything there is to know about running the organization. But it had to be someone I could trust... someone who shared my passion... someone with a profound understanding of what the Sticks meant to me. These were the non-negotiables. If I could find this person, I was confident I could shape them into a formidable powerhouse, able to manage this behemoth without me around every day.

Everyone I thought about bringing on board only wanted to talk about baseball. But baseball was the easy part of this job. I didn't need a coach.

I also didn't want someone who had their own vision of what they thought Sticks baseball could become. I already had the vision; I needed someone who could take that vision… and share it with anyone who wanted to talk about summer baseball… someone with great communication skills who was organized and trustworthy. I needed a Sticks ambassador.

In late 2020, I finally convinced Evan Hamm to leave his HR job and become the Director of Baseball and the first full-time employee in the Sticks organization while I assumed the role of President. Not long after, we hired Hall of Fame high school coach Kyle Slayton as Vice President and Jeff Sullivan from Massachusetts to be the Director of National Teams.

I hadn't planned on adding three full-time employees in less than eighteen months, and truthfully, it cut into the profits. But it was worth every penny because the expansion has allowed me to pursue other projects like writing this book and starting "The Chase Brewster Show" podcast. Most importantly, it has allowed me to engage more in what I really love — helping players reach the college level and planning for the future of Sticks Baseball.

For a long time, baseball consumed my life, even though I had other hobbies and dreams. Before I knew it, I had built something impossible for one person to sustain. Now, Evan Hamm handles all calls, texts, and emails and runs the back end of Sticks Baseball. Kyle Slayton started coaching in more national events and was available in the fall for the big October events since he was no longer coaching football. Jeff Sullivan was able to take our national teams and players to another level.

We would later add Jamarkus James as our General Manager in charge of licensing Sticks franchises in other states, Cory Lambert as Director of Player Personnel, Matt McAdoo as Director of Player Lodging, and Brett Usrey as Director of Player Advancement. It took almost nine years, but we finally have a full staff on salary, allowing me to fill the role of the President, monitor my staff, and fill in when needed.

Don't get me wrong – I still work hard, but I work hard at the stuff that I am good at and enjoy doing. My days no longer consist of taking phone calls or filling rosters so that our twenty-five teams will be eligible to play. Now I can spend my time doing what I love and changing the world in the best way that I know how— talking to colleges, being a mentor, creating content, traveling, and anything else that excites me.

The point is that you should be selfish with your time. Hire people who can do the tasks you are not good at or don't want to do so you can spend your time doing what you love. I am a firm believer that there is nothing wrong with saying, "I don't want to do it." *You* don't have to do everything yourself; just find a way to get it done. Most importantly, hire the best people to help grow the business.

This concept became clear to me recently when my wife Alisha and I were on vacation at Disney World in Orlando. For the first 33 years of my life, I had been to Disney zero times. In the last year, we went five times. We are definitely making up for lost time. During one visit, we were on a roller coaster, and my watch would not stop buzzing mid-ride. When the ride ended, I looked to see what could have been so important for such a large number of texts in such a short time. A parent, not the player, had added me to a group message with nine unknown numbers asking for donations to one of our player's high school baseball programs. Several others in the group were asking random questions and liking the original message, so I removed myself from the group.

If a parent asks me for donations instead of the player, I automatically ignore it. Also, I won't donate to anyone who randomly puts ten strangers in a group message instead of taking the time to send ten individual messages. However, if I like the player and the parents, I have no problem with them asking me to support their son's baseball program, just not in a group message while I am at Disney World.

Later that day, Alisha and I were still at the park, and I got a text from the mom saying she was offended that I had left the group message. I explained to her why I did it, and she apologized for any inconvenience.

The following week, the player posted a video on Twitter and tagged another summer program in the caption. So, not only did I have to deal with this drama during my vacation, but I also had to come home and deal with a player leaving the Sticks because I upset his mom by leaving her unsolicited group message.

I texted the mom about the situation, and she told me again that she was disappointed that I left the group message and that she felt her son should play somewhere else in the summer. It was probably for the best… can you imagine three years of dealing with a person who becomes so upset that someone on vacation with their family would be selfish with their time? Somehow, this made me the bad guy in her mind.

## Curiosity

At the end of the day, you will always be something to someone —a son, daughter, husband, wife, coach, teacher, or grandparent. The most important thing is that you can be saved. Then, in my opinion, you must be curious, creative, and committed. Find time to do these three things daily because your business depends on curiosity, creativity, and commitment as much as it depends on being selfish with your time.

Curiosity about all aspects of your business can be the difference between being cutting edge and setting trends or staying afloat by following trends. Ask questions like "What makes this work the way it does," or "Why did this marketing campaign fail?" Be curious about the wording of your campaigns, which fonts you use, and your letter sizing. Don't say, "It has always been done this way," and settle for mediocre results.

What will your business look like one year from now? Five years from now? How did a competitor go to market with a new product before you? There is always a reason. It could be that your competitors have better or more resources than you do. If they have equipment or software that you do not have, you can fix that quickly. But you can't fix something you don't know is broken, so always be curious enough to ask yourself why things are the way they are.

Consider the story of Kameron Forte's dad, Ike Forte, who played in the NFL for the New England Patriots, New York Giants, and the Washington Redskins. Before the NFL, Ike had a Hall of Fame career at the University of Arkansas. As a running back for the Razorbacks, he wore the number 85 on his jersey. You don't often hear about a running back wearing a number over thirty-nine if that high.

My obsession with branding made me curious. So, I finally asked him what was significant about the number 85 that he would use it for such an important part of his identity. It turns out that the University of Alabama had a running back who wore a number in the 80s, and Ike liked how it looked on him in the backfield. He thought that player stood out, and he wanted to stand out as well. It's as simple as that. Sometimes, things we are curious about have simple explanations. So, anytime you see a picture of Razorback Hall of Famer Ike Forte wearing number 85, you'll know how it came about.

If you are reading this, you are probably familiar with Jeff Petty, owner and founder of Canes Baseball. The Canes wore orange and green uniforms before making a deal with Evo Shield that required them to wear their now iconic black and yellow color scheme. When interviewing Jeff on my podcast, I asked him how he came up with his original color scheme, something I know a lot of people in our industry are curious about. It was as simple as he and a friend watched the Miami Hurricanes play one weekend and he liked how the colors looked.

The more questions you ask to satisfy your curiosity, the more data and information you will gain to help in your life, in business, and in getting to know others. This could be as simple as asking someone, "If you could have dinner with five people, dead or alive, who would they be?" (In case you're wondering... my five guests would be John Calipari, Elon Musk, Martin Luther King, Jr., LeBron James, and Walt Disney.)

## Creativity

Creativity is an important trait to possess because you could use it to help get your business out of a difficult situation. For example, if you have an entire warehouse of inventory you can't sell, some creative rebranding and marketing could help you sell that inventory in no time. Creative marketing can change your entire business overnight, like Nike did with "Just Do It" or the dairy industry with "Got Milk." These slogans were simple, yet effective enough to generate billions in sales.

On the other hand, bad marketing campaigns that lack creativity can cost you, like when American Airlines introduced AAirpass in the early 1980s and lost millions. It was lazy and uncreative marketing. Just as was the "New Coke" marketing campaign by Coca-Cola introduced in 1985.

The right creative team can turn everyday things into a staple for your business, which is exactly what graphics designer Blaine Tanner did for the Sticks. Our graphics department has always been leaps and bounds ahead of our competitors, but none more than basic lineup graphics. The Sticks are known to change our lineup graphic on social media every couple of weeks. We have replicated the University of Arkansas, professional teams, and anything else we can draw inspiration from. Last summer, our Chicago White Sox Scout Team used a Chicago White Sox replica graphic design.

I knew from the start that we would need likes, retweets, and impressions to grow the program on social media. So, I made sure we posted lineup graphics on Twitter for every game. Each player's parents, friends, girlfriends, high school programs, family members, etc., would retweet the lineup graphic for every game of the summer.

We also followed up every game, win or lose, with a post-game tweet tagging the game's top performers and including a video of some top plays, creating more opportunities for impressions on our Sticks account. I was smart enough to know we needed to post pre- and post-game information to the world, and I was creative enough to do it using graphics and videos.

The Sticks' creativity has always been one step ahead and is showcased in how we market our gear. For example, we offer new gear to players and families every few months. We also have a *Shirt of the Month* club, where we offer one or two new shirts that are available during that month only and will never be reprinted for sale. The Sticks family can't get enough of these.

Our gear is shipped in a custom Sticks bag that is labeled "Sticks Mystery Package" with our logo. We got the idea for the bags from the Savannah Bananas. They take it a step further by wrapping everything in yellow tissue paper and shipping merchandise in yellow boxes stamped with "Delivered Fresh."

Let me share a crazy story about how on-point the Savannah Bananas branding is. Recently, Jesse Cole and the Savannah Bananas team sent me a gift box. My wife and I had just moved, so I had to pick up the package at the post office later in the week. The employee helping me said, "It's a good thing you came in. We planned to throw this away if you did not show up today because the fresh fruit will start to rot."

Their branding was so good that a post office employee thought the yellow box containing Banana-themed baseball items contained actual bananas. Little did she know, it was a signed Jesse Cole Bananas jersey and baseball, as well as a nice handwritten note that I was very grateful to receive.

This is another reminder to be creative with things you are already doing, as it will mean more to your fans and customers. Something as simple as packaging can make your product stand out.

The best advice I can give, and the first step to running a successful business, is to be selfish with your time. Time is currency, and it is the one thing you can never get back. The minute you have room in your budget, hire people who can be extensions of yourself. Free yourself up to have time to change the world and enjoy doing what you love to do.

Along the way, countless distractions will tempt you to become something else, or even worse, someone else. It's crucial to sidestep these distractions because the latest trends will fade and be replaced by new ones. Disgruntled co-workers, relationship issues, raising children—you name it—all can obstruct your path to your dreams. You'll encounter people who believe you work too hard, or not hard enough, and all opinions in between. What truly matters is that you know, deep within, that you've given your all to realize your dreams.

Selfishness, curiosity, and creativity are traits that can forever change your business and your life.

# The Importance of Your Mentorship Circle

*"Without vision, how will you know what success looks like?"*
– Pat Williams

Achieving success takes a village—family, friends, teachers, idols, business partners—you name it. They all play a huge part in your business's success, but none more so than your mentors.

Few people have ever gotten to where they are now without being surrounded by like-minded people. You've probably heard Jim Rohn's quote: "You are the average of the five people you spend the most time with." I wholeheartedly believe that, and I also believe that the future success of your business can be forecasted as the sum of the five people in your mentorship circle.

## Mentors and Mentorship Circles

Many people in your life can take on the role of mentor: a parent who gives you advice every day, a co-worker you see every day, or even someone you have never met but you can read books and watch numerous documentaries about their life, like Martin Luther King, Jr. or Walt Disney.

Most great mentors have written work you can reference when you are unsure about a business philosophy or a podcast you can listen to when you are wondering where your industry is headed next. The great thing about being a Christian is that the Word is always available to you when you need to know what to do. While I would never compare the word of a business mentor to the Word of Jesus Christ, it is the same principle. A mentor's word is there to follow when you need to make good decisions. Not every person will have one-on-one access to those they look up to, so audio, video, and written work go a long way in helping shape your business plans and dreams.

Some people play with an extra card in their mentorship circle deck. I am a firm believer that having five people in your circle is as important as your business plan itself. I also believe your significant other is your plus one in the circle. In my case, there would be no Sticks Baseball without my beautiful wife, Alisha. Our pastor likes to say that she is the string to my balloon.

I guess you could say I got the "Cheat Code" to be lucky enough to spend almost every second of my day with Alisha. She knows the ins and outs of the Sticks better than I do. I run every idea, uniform design, and roster and lineup change by her to get her opinion. She is a great judge of character and is never afraid to tell me that I am not as funny or famous as I think I am. I truly hope you have someone you can trust with your business decisions who can answer without prejudice like my wife can—not someone who is looking for a promotion or is worried about getting fired. Someone who can tell you immediately whether something is a good idea or not, and you know it is their truth. Marrying Alisha was the best decision I have ever made, and it has taken our business to new heights without adding an employee salary.

One extra benefit of writing this book was being able to put my theories to the test. It is one thing to think enough of yourself to write about being successful; it is another thing to confirm that the five people in your mentorship circle reflect good business decisions.

So, I'm going to share the five people in my mentorship circle, and it may surprise you who I've included. But first, I want to explain that I did not include my dad or my brother, although both could have easily been listed. If you are like me and have several people you could include in your circle, you are a very lucky person and businessman.

My dad, Dave Brewster, is the greatest guy I know. He allowed me to chase my dreams, even when everyone around him thought he was crazy for not making me get a "real job." My dad had his own production company called "Smokin' Productions" and was also a semi-famous DJ in the 1980s and 90s. He was one of the first people to book Garth Brooks outside of Nashville, TN, at the beginning of his career, as well as famous acts such as Travis Tritt and Sawyer Brown.

Dad realized the importance of networking, even before it was considered *networking*, by working side by side with top agents and managers out of Nashville. He did things thirty years ago that today it is difficult to comprehend the magnitude of the moments.

For example, he would consider highway laws in his outlaw planning. Truck drivers were legally required to take mandatory breaks after driving a certain distance. When leaving Nashville and going to Dallas, Texarkana was the optimal place for truck drivers to stop and rest. Dad figured why not offer complimentary hotel rooms and paying jobs for shows if they were going to be in Texarkana anyway? The results could not have been better.

Unfortunately, I never got to see him really work in his field or see his passion on full display. When I started elementary school, he and Kevin West had the number one morning show at KTAL – FM 98 Rocks in Shreveport, LA. Every day, my dad would drive over an hour to work, leaving at 3 am. He would have to rush back to pick me up from school at 2:30 every day because most days, my mom would be too drunk to pick me up. Eventually, he chose his kids and family over his career, something I know had to be miserable for him. He left the music production industry to sell cars. At 63, despite many health problems, he still goes to work every day with the mindset of "Don't do anything to let them think they don't need me." His work ethic truly is amazing.

I also could have easily added my brother, Dylan Brewster, to my mentorship circle. I send every graphic, uniform design, and promotion rollout to him first because it's important to have someone outside of your industry whom you can trust to provide feedback on your ideas. The Sticks puts such an emphasis on being a baseball company that we forget some parents or grandparents may not have played baseball or don't know the lingo. Running these by Dylan gives us an honest opinion from a non-baseball lifer, allowing us to focus on colors, fonts, and other artistic features before posting for the world to see.

Dylan has made a living being a salesman. At 25, he was running his own Champs Sports four plus hours away from home. He eventually moved to Key West, FL, to run his own liquor store, doing everything from placing the alcohol and liquor orders to opening the store every morning. He currently works for Decker Sports, on his way to becoming one of their top salesmen.

Again, your mentorship circle does not have to include only millionaires or people you think have a good resume. I could have easily added my dad and brother to my list because I trust their opinions, and their voice matters to me.

## Types of Mentors

My mentorship circle can be divided into three categories: idol, hero, or role model. The mentors in each category impact my life differently. You may have access to some mentors in your circle and can communicate when needed. Others can change your life through social media clips, quotes, and books.

### Role Models, Heroes, and Idols

An Idol is someone who is admired, loved, or respected, such as a football player or a movie star, according to the Cambridge Dictionary. A Role Model is defined by Webster as a person whose behavior in a particular role is imitated by others. A Hero is just that, someone who means the world to you.

The five role models, heroes, and idols who comprise my mentorship circle are listed below. I wish you luck as write your list of those who have greatly impacted your life. Hopefully, like me, you have a circle that is overflowing with the greatest people you could ask for.

**Steve Landers, Jr., Role Model** – It would be hard for me to use the word mentor and not mention Steve. I have been fortunate to spend so much time around one of the state's most successful people, who has become like a second dad to me. In Arkansas, Steve's family is synonymous with success and car dealerships. Steve followed in his dad's footsteps, making his own path in the family business before moving on to other business ventures. For the longest time, I saw myself as just a baseball guy, and Steve helped me progress to the next level from a business standpoint.

Steve has included me in deals and goes out of his way to give me life advice daily. He is the force of everything I do off the field because he gave me the confidence to go after my dreams. I am forever grateful for our friendship. Our families have become very close. There may not be a player I loved or yelled at more than Tripp Landers. Steve and his wife, Karmen, also have two beautiful daughters, Aubree and Annika. Thank you, Steve, for everything!

**Jesse Cole, Idol** – I have spoken with Jesse a few times, but I still consider him an idol. He is the owner of the Savannah Bananas, which has taken over baseball right now. Jesse's book "Fans First" really changed my outlook on what "success" meant. Without his vision for changing the way baseball treats its fans, you would not be reading this.

I am so thankful to have had him on my podcast as our Season Three finale guest, which was also a highlight for me to interview my idol. I am forever indebted to him for that and have told him such. I have met many people through baseball, but I only have four jerseys hanging in my office, and that is by choice.

1. Logan O'Hoppe — the first Sticks player to play in the major leagues with the Los Angeles Angels of Anaheim.

2. Masyn Winn's St. Louis Cardinal powder blue jersey (former Sticks player).

3. Jonathan Ornelas's white Texas Rangers (former Sticks player).

4. Yellow Savannah Bananas jersey signed by Jesse Cole.

Jesse has had that kind of impact on my career. He will tell you his idols are Walt Disney, PT Barnum, and Bill Veeck, none of whom he has met. His podcast and interviews have also been a breath of fresh air that allows me to stay one step ahead of everyone in my baseball world. Most importantly, he taught me how to give our players and parents an A+ experience, and for that, I say thank you, Jesse!

**Kameron Forte, Role Model** – Kameron and I have been best friends for more than fifteen years, and he was the best man at my wedding. Kameron married his beautiful wife, Shallon, and adopted her two children before welcoming another daughter, Piper. Kameron runs our Sticks Softball program—his oldest daughter Callie is a very talented softball player. Last summer, we were lucky to finally have Kameron coach with me as he joined our White Sox Scout Team coaching staff and was invaluable in the dugout.

Having someone in your organization who knew you before you achieved success and has seen you at your worst is critical. I ensure Kameron is involved in my day-to-day decisions because I can tell immediately from his response if I am in the wrong. You cannot put a value on our friendship. I am excited to see how he will grow Sticks Softball and to watch the careers his daughters have in the sport.

Kameron will tell you that he has not always been perfect, but that is the power of growth. His dad, Ike Forte, played in the NFL for four years for the New England Patriots, Washington Redskins, and the New York Giants. His mom, Glenda Forte, was a very successful nurse. Kameron was a great athlete growing up and was drafted by the Los Angeles Dodgers. His career did not play out the same way his dad's did, but his success off the field will be just as impactful. I am thankful for everything we have built in the past fifteen years and excited to see what the next fifteen years look like. Thank you, Kam!

**LeBron James, Idol** – Like any other mid-thirties sports-loving guy, LeBron can do no wrong in my eyes. Although it is no surprise that LeBron is on the list, he made the list for reasons you may not have guessed. One of the most important things to me is ensuring my circle of family and friends is taken care of for life. LeBron has kept his circle of friends from his childhood close to him.

Rich Paul is his agent, hiring him when he had no experience. Mav Carter is the CEO of their businesses together. They have done so many great ventures together like Spring Hill Productions and Uninterrupted. Randy Mims is LeBron's right-hand man, and they are so close that LeBron has had different teams put him on payroll to be around the team in an everyday capacity. Brian Windhorst wrote a book about their circle and the roles everyone played called "LeBron, Inc.," which I read once a year to keep what is important at the forefront of my personal goals. In this case, his vision is my vision. When naming my LLC, I even chose "Brewster, Inc." to follow in his footsteps. It only felt right. There are so many reasons to love LeBron and possibly a few reasons to hate him, but I will forever be thankful for the blueprint he created that shows me how to keep what is important in perspective. Thank you, LBJ!

**Dirk Kinney, Role Model/Hero** – Let me start by saying there are very few people in this world who can make everyone around him do better and want better for themselves without trying. I would be lying if I said Dirk and I agreed on everything, mostly because he is old enough to be my dad. Several times a day, I make him mad, and I promise you that he will say the same about me. That is the beauty of it though. He pushes you to be the best version of yourself, even on your worst days. Putting the hero label on someone you talk to every day may seem like a bit much, but I have also never been around someone who cared about so many people and was respected by so many people in return. There is nothing I do in my day-to-day business life that I do not run by Dirk. Sometimes, I run my personal life decisions by him, too. He was a groomsman at our wedding and will undoubtedly play a huge role in my mentorship circle for years to come.

Dirk is a scout for the St. Louis Cardinals and has coached with the Sticks since the early days. He's been in the dugout, on the field, and at the hotels with all our players. When rumor was Masyn Winn would end up at the University of Arkansas instead of signing in the MLB Draft like originally projected, Dirk stood up and said Masyn was one of the greatest kids we have ever been around, you must take him. When others were saying Tink Hence's velocity was down, Dirk pulled out page after page of notes from the summer to prove otherwise. He had seen every pitch thrown for the last 18 months from Tink and told his bosses so.

Winn, Hence, Jaden Hill, Mateo Gil, Kurtis Bryne, Xavier Casserilla, Brycen Mautz, and Jordan Walker all played on the Rawlings National Scout Team/Sticks combo team at Jupiter, and were all drafted by the Cardinals. The Sticks cannot thank Dirk enough for all he does for us and our players, and I cannot thank him enough for the man that he has made me become. This book would not have been written if it were not for Dirk pushing me to be a better person. He was the first one to confront me about my weight and my diet, telling me in the nicest way possible that I had to change, or I was going to live a short life. We all need people who care enough to say something like that in our lives. Thank you, Dirk!

The five individuals in my mentorship circle, plus a few others, helped make me a better person. I challenge you to write down your five. If you can do that and be proud of your list, chances are you are running or involved in a very successful business.

Additionally, there are others I admire who embody these qualities. For instance, John Calipari, the head basketball coach at Kentucky, and Deion Sanders, the head football coach at Colorado, inspire me. I regularly seek out their content because it motivates me to improve as a coach, husband, and person. Identify individuals you respect, whether they are idols, heroes, or role models, and do a deep dive into their platforms and available content for motivation.

## Changing Mentor Circles

It is also worth noting that your mentor circle will change over time based on who you are around every day. My list at 34 is not the same as it was at 18. Since I was around Will Bolt and Justin Seely every day when I was 18, they most likely would have been inside my circle then.

Without Coach Seely teaching me how to recruit and communicate with potential players, there would be no Sticks Baseball. He gave me the drive and knowledge to make sure each team had the best players. Without Coach Bolt teaching me how to be organized and plan everything to the second, there would be no Sticks Baseball. Coach Seely and Coach Bolt gave me a masterclass on running a Division 1 program as a guy who would never be talented enough to be a part of a D1 program.

So many people who I talk to daily, like Kyle Slayton, Tim Decker, Kyle Davis, Tyler Sawyer, Scott Mennie, Jonathan Gosdin, Morgan Smith, Tanner Rockwell, Shaun Manning, and many others, flow in and out of my circle at any given time. I am so thankful for the input and love they return to me. I also talk to community staples, like our Pastor, Brother Tim Montgomery weekly, who at times are inside the circle to ensure I am making the right decisions in my life. I seriously cannot thank these guys enough.

Your mentorship circle will continuously evolve. Each person in your circle that you mentor will become a mentor for someone else. One of the best parts of my job is helping younger coaches grow and being there to help them figure out life and business on their journey. Make sure you are doing your part to keep your circle interlocked and give back to others' circles as well.

# Pillar #3

# To Be Great, You Must
# Be Uncomfortable

*"The best lessons you learn are the ones you
never realize are being taught to you"*
– Kendra Scott

In a sport where most coaches look like they can still play, even fifteen years past their prime, I've always stood out for the wrong reasons. Only I could fall in love with one of the few sports where coaches dress like players. Unlike other sports, if you weren't skilled as a player, it can really be a hurdle for you as a baseball coach, especially when throwing batting practice and hitting ground balls with a Fungo bat.

There is nothing more uncomfortable for a plus-size guy than wearing a full Chicago White Sox uniform while coaching in the biggest events of the year in a sport he never really played.

There is always self-doubt. Do I look the part physically? Have I learned enough to pass the information on to our players or employees? Coaching is as stressful and communication intensive as it gets.

The joy and passion I have for what I do and for our players will always surpass my fear of embarrassment. When you love something and are in it for the right reasons, you will figure out the rest. You can do like I did and lose close to eighty pounds to change your body to look the part. You can attend every game, clinic, and convention and be part of every conversation to learn as much as possible about your profession. You can find a way to beat that uncomfortable feeling only to move to the next phase of your career and have that uncomfortable feeling again.

## Ignore the Noise

Success is a two-way street, and I'm watching a lot of cars going in the other direction. I can pinpoint the moment I felt like Sticks had finally "made it." You know you've reached a peak when social media erupts—not everyone rejoices in your achievements. Countless times, I've seen tweets subtly targeting me, yet conspicuously omitting my name. Nothing is more uncomfortable than personal attacks stemming from others' resentment toward your successful business.

These challenges only fuel my determination. I'm tempted to retaliate, like poaching their players or undermining their brand instead of responding to them directly. Dirk and Ced always tell me there is power in not acknowledging such pettiness, something magical about not giving someone the time or day or acting like you did not notice their child-like behavior.

Once, a parent told me that travel baseball feels a lot like WWE, and they were right. Not everyone signed up for the fun and games that come along with the actual games. I have frequently addressed something that was said online in person or through text like an adult, and the response was as if we both knew the script before that week's episode started. I am the most non-confrontational guy there is, but I just do not understand the "let's bash Brewster and the Sticks to gain followers" logic. Either we like each other or we don't. I am not in the mindset of acting like we don't like each other on social media, then in real life, we will speak and shake hands.

I made a vow to myself to avoid all internet drama, no matter how petty or untrue the attempt to assassinate my character. I know we have the best product in the state for my industry. The Sticks have elevated from a regional program to a national program, so we're too focused to entertain the drama. Over the years, I have let hundreds of messages full of hate go without a response. Each message felt like the onset of a conflict, but I would simply take a screenshot, saved them, and move on. I could not tell you what any of those tweets said today, but the images are somewhere on my phone.

## Jupiter

One of The Sticks' greatest moments came when we finally earned a bid for the biggest event of the year: the 18U World Wood Bat Association Tournament. Hosted by Perfect Game each October in West Palm Beach, FL, at the St. Louis Cardinals and Miami Marlins Spring Training facility, this event is the pinnacle in the amateur baseball world. Although commonly referred to as Jupiter, since it's technically played in Jupiter, FL, its official name carries significant weight. It's the most challenging event to get into and undoubtedly the most prestigious. For our first six years of attending Jupiter, we partnered with Coach Manning and his teams for this event. The expenses to play in this event are staggering, and this alliance gave our players the best shot at playing in Jupiter.

Initially, we played in the event as the "Miami Marlins Scout Team," and it was so much fun representing the Marlins on the field. This encouraged me to set a goal to one day represent a Major League Team co-branded with The Sticks.

However, once Derek Jeter took over the Marlins, we had to change our name to the "Rawlings National Scout Team." Soon after, Perfect Game extended an invitation for us to attend as the Sticks, but I chose to stay with Coach Manning's group as long as possible. Eventually, Perfect Game required us to change the team's name to "Rawlings National Scout Team/Sticks." In hindsight, this was a significant and positive milestone for us.

In 2021, we left the nest and played in the event as "3n2 Sticks Baseball 18U Brewster" for the first time, and it was such an awesome experience. In 2022, we finally reached our goal of representing an MLB team, going to Jupiter as the "3n2 Sticks Baseball 18U Brewster/White Sox Scout Team," wearing the same MLB uniforms the White Sox wore.

Our local newspaper captured this moment with an article emphasizing the importance of attending this event for our program and the excitement it brought to the event. The week was a high point for our program, players, and the state of Arkansas.

In the three years since we started playing in Jupiter as the Sticks/White Sox Scout Team, we've consistently been a strong contender. We were predicted to win our pool each year and were twice favored to win the event. Making the playoffs twice, we have forged as many memories as possible for a group of 25 players and coaches in a five-day tournament.

There was initial apprehension about participating as the Sticks without the co-branding of the Rawlings National Team. Yet, this challenge allowed us to stand on our own, showcasing our strongest play in the most prestigious tournament we've faced.

## Focus on the Positives

On the road to doing something great, not everyone will be happy for you, even people you love and respect. While you cannot control how others feel, you can turn uncomfortable situations into great moments. This was particularly evident when we faced our toughest challenge: backlash on social media from individuals we respected.

In the initial draft of this book, I detailed instances where individuals who we respect sought to discredit our program's achievements on social media. By the final draft, these accounts were omitted. Recognizing that drama attracts attention, I also acknowledged that maturity entails demonstrating exemplary behavior in managing conflicts, and that is exactly what we did over time. Despite their attempts on social media, we soon experienced some of the most financially successful months in our program's history.

This shift happened almost overnight. Our players and parents were incredibly receptive to our new initiatives, especially one that we launched the following week. We introduced the "Sticks Mystery Package," which immediately captivated our audience, selling out in its first two months of offering. On the first Monday of each month, we released an exclusive, never-before-seen t-shirt, accompanied by two mystery items, ranging from Sticks-themed bracelets and pens to ornaments and cups.

## The Chase Brewster Show

Ironically, the aspects of my career that people enjoy the most have been uncomfortable moments for me. For over four years, I shared with my wife and friends my desire to start a podcast, but my insecurities about my teeth, my weight, and my accent made the idea of becoming a podcast star improbable. Yet I knew I had a compelling story to share and a platform to do it.

The concept for the podcast initially emerged in 2019 when Kyle Slayton, Cederick Harris, Jr., and I were driving to Little Rock, AR for a meeting. That day was filled with shared stories and laughter, and a social media post about our trip sparked interest from our community. Friends expressed wishes to have been part of our conversations, saying things like, "Man, I wish I could have been a fly on that wall," indicating a potential audience for such content.

I started sharing my vision about starting a podcast with them. I was certain it would be a hit. Podcasts were somewhat new at this time, and Kyle did not see the point in doing it and was concerned it would be too time-consuming. Ced is a private guy by nature and does not want to let the world into his private life.

I knew it would work, so I considered replacing them but struggled to recreate the chemistry we had in Little Rock. Then, when someone in our hometown launched a similar concept on Facebook Live, I worried about being perceived as a copycat. Everything pointed to an uncomfortable situation, so it was easier to shelf the podcast.

During these years, I periodically revisited the idea, adjusting the vision and potential collaborators, but never quite finding the right formula. Finally, in August 2022, I took a leap of faith and decided to launch the podcast solo. Announcing "The Chase Brewster Show" was a bold move, especially considering I had no equipment, guests, or experience.

Talk about being uncomfortable. At this point, I was scared to death. I had posted on every social media platform, so there was no turning back now. The day I recorded the first episode was filled with anxiety. I had to push back the start time and run to BestBuy to buy a new microphone that would cover my mouth and teeth.

Despite how uncomfortable I was when the day started, Episode One with Dirk Kinney of the St. Louis Cardinals was a huge success. Almost an hour after we posted, Willie Prince, a social media mastermind, sent me a text saying, "I see you are at 80 views, that's great. My first YouTube video had 80 views in total. It's hard at first with no subscribers."

The next morning, to my surprise, the episode had soared to over 900 views, far exceeding my expectations. This was a clear sign that, despite my discomfort and fear, starting my show was not only rewarding but also a success.

In its first season on YouTube, each episode of The Chase Brewster Show surpassed one thousand views. The momentum continued in Season Two, which we launched on Apple Podcasts and Spotify, surpassing all expectations and garnering over 30,000 streams. Now, in Season Three, the podcast has evolved into a platform for engaging conversations with influential figures in the sports industry.

I've had the privilege to interview some of my closest friends in the industry, like LSU Head Coach Jay Johnson, Nebraska Head Coach Will Bolt, Texas State Head Coach Steven Trout, Arkansas Little Rock Head Coach Chris Curry, and Georgia Head Coach Wes Johnson.

The podcast has also allowed me to connect with respected individuals outside my immediate network, such as Savanah Bananas owner Jesse Cole, Baseballism CEO Travis Chock, Colorado Athletic Director Rick George, and ELAC Head Basketball Coach and "Last Chance U" star John Mosley Jr. These interviews not only added diversity to the show but also allowed me to form new, meaningful connections.

I have yet to listen to one word of my podcast. I record the episodes, save them, and send them to my brother for an initial review. Then, he sends them to Blaine Tanner for editing before he releases them to the world. The positivity and enthusiasm in the feedback I get in texts and comments often surprise me.

One Christmas, Alisha surprised me with a custom hoodie that said, "The Chase Brewster Show" with my face on it. When I shared a photo of me wearing the hoodie online, the response was unexpected and overwhelming. Many people reached out, expressing their desire to purchase one. This attention was somewhat uncomfortable but in a good way.

The success of Season One of "The Chase Brewster Show" would not have been possible without the invaluable contributions of our guests, to whom I am immensely grateful. Each guest brought their unique perspectives and insights, enriching the content and appeal of the show. I extend my deepest thanks to Dirk Kinney of the St. Louis Cardinals, Willie Prince from Black Cobra Media, Noah Sanders, assistant baseball coach at the University of Arkansas - Little Rock, Todd Schaefer, the women's basketball coach at the University of Arkansas, Olivia Shepperd of Shepard Law Firm, Jacob Capels, baseball coach at Southern Arkansas University, Jheremy Brown, a scout with Perfect Game, and Savannah Alaniz of the Savannah Bananas. Their contributions went far beyond just being guests; they were instrumental in shaping the show into what it became, and for that, my gratitude to each of them is endless.

Seasons Two and Three have also featured incredible guests, including Derek Simmons, one the most respected coaches in college baseball. After our episode, he said, "You have a natural flow for being on a podcast, my man. Follow your dreams and your passion." His comments meant the world to me because he had no idea how uncomfortable I was during the show.

## Writing a Book

Embarking on the journey of writing this book has been an uncomfortable process for me. There's a constant uncertainty: not knowing if anyone will find value in it, or if the time and effort I've poured into it will ultimately be worthwhile. However, I am also smart enough to know the book's potential impact cannot be realized if I don't write it. Stepping out of my comfort zone is the only way I can motivate and help change the world.

If this book encourages one person to slide into that uncomfortable lane and do something great, its purpose will be fulfilled. I challenge you to confront your fears and embark on your life goal which is just outside your comfort zone. I wish you luck finding success and moving on to something new and uncomfortable.

Throughout our journey, both personally and as part of the Sticks, we have encountered numerous uncomfortable situations that seemed like insurmountable roadblocks.

These challenges often felt unnecessary or daunting at the time but have invariably transformed into blessings in hindsight. It's a common misconception that uncomfortable moments are there to halt progress. In reality, they are the very catalysts that propel us toward success.

It's important to recognize that true greatness emerges from discomfort. Only when we confront and move beyond these uneasy moments can we reach new heights of success. However, with each new level achieved, it's typical to encounter further challenges. This is the nature of growth and greatness – a continuous cycle of facing and overcoming discomfort.

So, the message is clear: embrace the uncomfortable. It's a sign that you're on the path to something great. Overcoming these moments isn't just part of the journey; it's essential to it. Go forth, face these challenges head-on, and achieve the greatness that awaits.

# Pillar #4

# Look For Greatness in Everything You Do

*"You become what you think about."*
– Abe Lincoln

Anything worth doing at the highest level comes with a price. Leadership is challenging, and teaching leadership principles is just as hard. I can share what has worked for me, but everyone has different backgrounds and experiences, so what I did may not work for you. The question is: what price are you willing to pay to reach your goals?

Looking at athletes who get paid millions of dollars, we think they have it made in life. They can afford anything and access exclusive entertainment or sporting events. However, their personal sacrifices are seldom discussed. A major league baseball player plays 162 games per season, with at least 82 road games, not to mention spring training. That's a lot of time away from their families. Is the financial compensation worth these personal sacrifices?

This mindset goes back to my habit of saying, "It could always be worse," when facing an unfavorable situation. I firmly believe that greatness is all around you, even in dire situations. The pandemic opened our eyes to just how great and precious life is.

The Sticks have always been ahead of the curve, dominating spaces others took for granted. When we first started, most other programs wore basic dri-fit t-shirts as "jerseys" and required players to bring their own pants. This detracted from the greatness these programs had built by drawing attention to the mismatched pants and ten-dollar shirts. The different colored helmets worn by players further diminished the team's aesthetic, especially in social media photos. These details, though small, significantly impacted the perception of greatness.

From our first game in 2016, we went all out to promote greatness, finding the adage, "It does not cost much more to go first class" to be true. Pre-COVID, coaches carried team helmets to the games. However, with the introduction of CDC guidelines in 2020, we had each player order the same red helmet, at cost so he could use it for all four years of playing with Sticks. In 2022, we shifted to a white and black color scheme, but a supply shortage left us with an equipment shortfall for the first time since starting the program. Searching for greatness again, we proactively ordered 300 helmets from Decker in 2023 and included one in each player's uniform package, ensuring a consistent look among all players.

This is relevant because when we started the Sticks, our goal was to achieve greatness like other top programs. We spent hours in our office, strategizing around our whiteboard, aspiring to reach the heights of programs like the Canes or Banditos. Before even playing a game, we knew where we wanted to be. In 2016, the ultimate goal for players across the country was to play in a Perfect Game event. For your travel program to be recognized as a "big dog," you needed a featured Perfect Game article written about your team during an event. Perfect Game would typically publish one article per day, so, at an event like WWBA, 400-plus teams are fighting to be recognized in one of the five or six articles. It was a long shot, but that's how you find greatness.

## Separate Yourself

Our strategy to separate the Sticks from everyone else within the state and region revolved around three key elements. First, we focused on uniforms, choosing Majestic, the brand worn by Major League Baseball players at the time.

Second, we focused on scheduling since that was something we could control. Initially, our games were mostly played locally, often at nearby colleges, with occasional participation in Perfect Game events. Back then, traveling to five-to-seven-day events ten hours away was uncommon. We knew players wanted to compete in Perfect Game events, so we prioritized attending them. Before long, I was driving players to Atlanta and Phoenix. We had to play in as many of their events as possible to generate the social media clips and articles the players wanted.

Our debut at a Perfect Game event earned us a prominent front-page article, which at the time was one of our "we made it" moments. The highlight of this achievement was seeing an article on the Perfect Game website and a picture of Hunter Watson (Texas A&M), Kaleb Hill (Ole Miss), Connor Noland (Arkansas), and myself standing together at Camelback Stadium in our red Sticks uniforms and navy SB hats.

A defining moment came during our first WWBA event when Jaden Hill came out of the bullpen for his first Perfect Game appearance, hitting 95 mph. Perfect Game's Instagram detailing Hill's performance had over 25,000 views overnight, eventually reaching over 80,000 views. This WWBA event was our definition of greatness, both from the on-field performance and social media standpoint.

What better way to begin our WWBA Playoff history than to play the number one team in the country, the Central Florida Gators? The Gators were one of the best put-together teams in PG history, and many of their players have achieved remarkable success in professional baseball. The 11th-ranked player in the country, PG All-American and first-rounder to the Washington Nationals, Mason Denaburg, hit lead-off. The third-ranked player in the country, PG All-American and St. Louis Cardinals future star Nolan Gorman hit in the three-hole. Toronto Blue Jays first-rounder Gunner Hoglund hit in the four-hole, with PG All-American and Cardinal 17th-rounder Elijah Cabell hitting behind him. 10th ranked player in the country, PG All-American and Cincinnati Reds third-rounder Tyler Callihan hit sixth for them, with PG All-American and Baltimore Orioles second-rounder Jud Fabian hitting behind him. PG All-American and New York Mets 25th-rounder Joe Charles hit ten hole for them to round out their lineup. What a lineup! 10 hitters, 6 PG All-Americans, and 7 MLB Draft picks.

To make things worse for us, they rolled out the number one player in the country, future Cardinals first-rounder, and PG All-American Matthew Liberatore as their starting pitcher. He would go three innings, five strikeouts, one walk, and no hits. The Gators also had Carter Stewart on their roster, another top talent ranked third in the country, a future first-round pick by the Atlanta Braves, and also a PG All-American, though we didn't face him. The Gators' roster was a testament to elite baseball talent: 20 players were Division 1 signees and many were future draft picks.

Despite losing the first game, the Sticks went on to defeat three teams that were ranked number one in the country by Perfect Game. Masyn Winn, Tink Hence, and Ethan Long combined to lead us to a victory over the Orlando Scorpions, whose lineup included future MLB talents Dylan Crews and Zac Veen.

We also beat the Brady House lead Team Elite Black in a 4-2 win at the PBR Showdown at Lakepoint in 2020 behind an incredible pitching performance by Colton Sims.

Our third win came as Jayson Jones walked with two outs in the first inning in 2021, followed by a Reese Robinett double and a Ty Waid triple to beat Canes National 2-1 at East Cobb. Sean Fitzpatrick was masterful on the mound to get the win.

## Getting Buy-In to A New Program

From the outset, we knew to be great we had to attract top talent. Convincing players to join the startup program was a challenge. We focused on what we could control: providing high-quality uniforms and a competitive schedule, hoping that would bring us great players.

Our efforts paid off when the first two players committed to our team: JaKobi Jackson, the top hitter in the state from Watson Chapel High School, and Connor Noland, the top pitcher in his class and a future standout at the University of Arkansas. I am forever grateful to their families for believing in our vision. Following their lead, the team rapidly grew with the addition of exceptional players such as Jaden Hill (LSU), Will Richardson (Arkansas State), Jaylen Deshazier (Arkansas State), Hayden Arnold (University of Arkansas – Little Rock), Colby Atkins (Abilene Christian), Bryson Haskins (Henderson State), Matt Aiken (Southern Arkansas), and many more great players.

For those outside the baseball industry, my business advice is to clearly define your primary objective, which for us was attracting top players. Consider what aspects are in your control to achieve your goal. We knew we could control uniforms, for instance. This included setting sub-goals to excel in preparation, mockups, color schemes, and timely delivery every year. By focusing on these details, we hoped to establish a benchmark so high that it becomes a challenge for other programs to match.

Finding greatness in everything we do involves a continuous and proactive search for inspiration. For example, Alisha and I visited the kid's section at the MLB store in Times Square New York despite not having children ourselves. One random shirt we ran across would inspire us to design something that would be one of our players' favorite items the following year. The pursuit of inspiration extends beyond just baseball. After every major sporting event or playoff game, we go through Fanatics pages online to look for more inspiration. I have a folder on my phone with over 300 screenshots of ideas for shirts, shorts, and jerseys. One of the best-selling items at 3n2 was something I designed for our players in the fall, and never thought about it again.

## Dealing with Loss

The tragic loss of Cedrick Harris Jr., affectionately known as CJ, a remarkable eighth-grade player in our program, has been deeply felt by our community. His father, Cedrick Harris, a close friend and former LSU baseball player and Arizona Diamondbacks athlete, and his mother, Marie Ferdinand-Harris, a WNBA veteran and LSU women's basketball Hall of Famer, are integral to our extended family.

It is impossible to find greatness in this situation, but we strive to honor CJ's greatness and his impact on those around him. We started by retiring his jersey number 24 across our entire program. We also started the #BeLikeCJ scholarship award. Thanks to the support of Stanley Wood, we were able to provide every Sticks player a jersey t-shirt featuring 'Sticks' on the front and 'Harris Jr. 24' on the back. We also sold these shirts available online, with all proceeds going to the Harris family.

CJ was one of the rare 8$^{th}$-grade baseball players who had been offered college scholarships. He had more than one offer, but the most important one was from his parent's alma mater, LSU.

In the summer following CJ's passing, we took additional steps to honor his memory and legacy. We introduced a special # BeLikeCJ-themed uniform for my Sticks team, adopting a purple and yellow LSU color scheme. Each jersey said Harris Jr. and 24 on the back. The players' numbers were on the front so the umpires knew who the players were. Other teams in our Sticks program wore jerseys with a logo on the sleeve that said CJ24 inside a baseball to honor him. Everywhere we went, we tried to honor CJ in any way we could. We did all we could to find greatness in this situation, even when it seemed there was none.

## Travel

It would be impossible for me to include a chapter about finding greatness in everything without talking about my traveling adventures. I am terrified to fly. I love to travel, but I fear heights, which is a bad combination. Whenever we fly, I tell myself, "You asked for this life," under my breath over and over. Our 2022 travel schedule was by far the most extensive, taking three flights to New York, Orlando, FL, Fort Myers, FL, Los Angeles, CA, and Phoenix, AZ.

One month, we took ten individual flights within two weeks. This is many miles of finding greatness in something that makes me feel far from great on the inside and is a perfect representation of my life. You have a guy who has dreams and goals that he wants to accomplish, while getting to travel the world with his family, but to do this, he has to face his biggest fear. I'm often asked how I overcame the fear of flying. I always say, "By flying as much as possible." Again, another representation of life.

In business, transforming setbacks into opportunities for greatness is crucial. This is the cheat code to life. It's easy to acknowledge success in its prime, but recognizing potential during challenging times is key. For example, now it is easy to say Michael Jordan was the greatest player ever. But who saw the greatness in him when he did not make his high school basketball varsity team as a sophomore?

Greatness in business is not limited to product quality; it extends to all facets, including promotion, communication, customer service, and even details like uniforms and packaging. The greatness in business applies to every part of your life. The smallest thing can change your brand and separate you from everyone else.

## Life is Art

Look for inspiration in everyday life, whether scrolling through Twitter or walking through a mall. Every aspect of life offers artistic inspiration, from fonts and colors to lighting. Everything the Sticks do to differentiate themselves—our approach to graphics, clothing, and presentation—is art.

Don't be afraid to find inspiration in your peers and competitors. For instance, Jeff Petty, the owner of the Canes, is someone I admire and seek advice from. In our industry, many seem to criticize him for having a dedicated bus for his players or a personal media crew. Instead of being jealous, I took the initiative. I asked 3n2 about getting our own bus, but apparently, insurance is a tough sell for a corporation. I believe if the COVID shutdown hadn't occurred, we would have a bus.

I also turn to other influential figures in baseball, such as Ray Delon of the Banditos, Mike Garciaparra of GBG, and Nelly Gonzales of FTB, for guidance. In this competitive field, despite rankings and rivalry, you must find greatness in the top-tier talent in your profession.

---

### There are no bad days.
### —Kevin Hart

---

Kevin Hart once said in an interview, "There are no bad days," and I couldn't agree more. I acknowledge that this perspective came easier after achieving a certain level of business and financial success. Sure, some days are filled with things I don't want to do, and some days are better than others, but there are no bad days. The Lord has blessed me with a beautiful wife and family, a business that allows us to leave a positive impact daily, and more money than we ever deserve. How could any day be a bad day under these circumstances?

I challenge you to truly reflect on how many bad days you have had. If you find that you've had more than a few 'bad days,' it might be time to reassess your daily routine and mindset. Life's too short for bad days.

I wish you luck in finding greatness in the smallest things because once you get that mindset, your business will take off and set you apart from everyone else. Unfortunately, when you become great at something, you will find that many people want to bring you down, which can be draining. Dirk Kinney always disagrees when I say, "Being successful is exhausting." Success often makes you a target, but the focus should always be on innovation and standing out—that's what greatness is.

# Pillar #5

# Share Your Struggles and Appreciate Your Success

*"Be yourself, everyone else is taken."*
– Oscar Wilde

It's important to know that struggling is okay and even expected. Success is challenging, often feeling like a rare achievement. The key point is that success is subjective. My definition may differ from yours, and that's completely acceptable.

We often hear, "I just want to be successful." However, what does being successful really mean for you? I think what people actually mean to say is "I want to be rich," or "I want to travel," or "I don't want to work anymore." Success is not a one-size-fits-all concept. We might not realize that we're already successful in someone else's eyes.

In today's world, the number of likes or retweets is available in real time, and there's a tendency to equate success with external validation. We tend to put too much pressure on ourselves based on how others define success – myself included. The old saying, "We buy things we do not want, with money we do not have, to impress people who we do not like" is so true.

61

My background and experiences are different from yours, so our visions of success may never align. Tim Decker, President and CEO of Decker Sports recently asked what I wanted out of life. After thinking about it for some time, I said, "I want to be able to buy anything I want without looking at the price or having to worry if I can afford it or not." Pointing at a coffee stand nearby, I said," If I wanted to buy you coffee, I don't care if it costs three dollars, or three hundred dollars for these two cups of coffee. If that is what is in my heart to do, I want to be able to buy you coffee, and not have to ask for the total."

I don't know whether that is a good answer or a bad answer, but it is *my* answer. Of course, I have other goals and even sub-goals, but that's my definition of success when someone asks me what I want out of life. I want to be able to create memories with great people without worrying about the electricity being shut off because I offered to buy something.

Success for me also means being able to take pride in something. We've won games 15-0, but there's not much pride in those match-ups. In those cases, it's hard for me to view that day as successful. Usually, it means we played below our standard, even though we were facing a team that was completely outmatched talent-wise. On the other hand, there have been countless games where we lost 2-1, but we played the best we possibly could that day in a competitive showdown. I always take great pride in games like that, knowing that it's been a successful day even in defeat. Unfortunately, in our sport, you can do everything right and still lose sometimes.

If I don't sell a single copy, this book will still be a success for me. If the Sticks don't win Jupiter or WWBA this year, it's still a successful summer. Doing things like playing in the toughest and biggest events or venturing out of my profession to write a book, hardly ever results in failure. The only failure I could face with this book is never putting it out there. I challenge you to think about what success means to you. Before we can appreciate our success, we must be comfortable sharing our struggles.

In chapter three, I talked about embracing discomfort. The odds were against me becoming the successful baseball coach you see today. No one could have predicted that an overweight kid who rarely played baseball and served as a high school team manager would turn his story into the success I share in this book. I struggled in school, like a lot of the kids in my friend group. I never felt like I wasn't smart or was held back a grade, but I can promise you it did not feel natural in the classroom. My first three semesters in college were a disaster; I did not pass a single class that would transfer. I went to class every day, was always polite, and never caused trouble, but still, I failed every class. If it weren't for this wonderful thing called "mini-mesters" and one summer when I took 27 hours from three different colleges, there would be no Sticks Baseball.

Fortunately, this story has a successful outcome. I graduated from two institutions I hold dear—Texarkana College and Texas A&M Texarkana—with degrees that make me a proud alumnus of both the Bulldogs and the Eagles.

In June 2023, Texarkana College honored me as Alumni of the Month, a recognition that meant a great deal to me. To follow that up, in October 2023, Texas A&M Texarkana awarded me the Distinguished Alumni Award. The Texas A&M Round Up banquet had not taken place since COVID, so there was a backlog of candidates. With four years' worth of alumni overlooked and limited spots available, there was some uncertainty on my part that I would be a winner. Even though I knew I was very deserving, I would tell myself all these things to prepare myself to cope with not getting selected or receiving that special phone call. Fortunately, my anxieties were put to rest when I received the congratulatory video from Morgan Smith and Brooklyn Jones.

Winning this award was high on my bucket list, and it truly meant so much to me. However, the award ceremony was scheduled during the school's homecoming week festivities and required me to accept the award in person on a Thursday, which happened to coincide with the biggest baseball event of the year in West Palm Beach, FL. Alisha and I rarely disagree, and I truly mean ever, but we were at odds on how to handle the situation.

Originally, I wanted to charter a private jet and attend both events. We would arrive in Florida on Tuesday for the baseball tournament, prepare for our two warm-up exhibition games on Wednesday, play an 8 AM game on Thursday, and then fly back to Texarkana. Although we are not wealthy by any means, I felt like chartering a plane was the only real way to make this work.

I've turned down several college baseball coaching offers over the years due to the timing, the location, or the current success of the Sticks and the inability to do both extremely well. However, there's one position I've had my eye on: leading the baseball program at my alma mater, Texas A&M Texarkana. This has been my dream job, even before they even started a program.

Not only was Texas A&M Texarkana my alma mater, but it was two miles from our new dream home and five minutes from

Alisha's mother's house. With the recent appointment of Dr. Ross C. Alexander as the new President of TAMUT, I knew this would be the perfect opportunity to introduce myself and make a good first impression. Steve Jones, the current TAMUT Head Baseball Coach, and a good friend of mine, is nearing retirement, so I wanted to plant the seed early with Dr. Alexander, and Michael Galvan, the school's Athletic Director.

Alisha and I compromised on a Thursday morning flight out of Fort Lauderdale. To make the flight, we had to leave before the game ended. Alisha made me promise to stay if the game was close. We scored another run in the top of the 7$^{th}$ inning to go up 4-1 against Canadian Premier. As I jogged off the field from coaching third base, Alisha and I jumped in Andrew Guerra's golf cart and headed to our car. Blake Baxendale drove us the one-hour drive to the airport. We arrived with barely any time to spare, carrying no luggage and still in my full baseball uniform.

We made it back to Texarkana in time. My dad had picked up my new suit, so we quickly changed and joined my family and friends for a memorable evening. At 5 AM on Friday, we were on our way back to Florida to make it in time for the evening game as if we had never left.

Recently, I decided to go back to school to pursue a master's degree. After receiving my BA in Criminal Justice, getting my MBA now made sense. I wanted to learn more about running a business the right way and avoid being taken advantage of during business meetings. My goal was to understand business operations firsthand, instead of relying on others' interpretations.

I started my first MBA class, Building Business Leaders, with Dr. Marcus Caster, in October at the University of Southern New Hampshire. So far, the program has been a perfect match for me, and I am on track to receive an A in the class.

To those reading this and contemplating furthering your education, either for personal satisfaction or professional advancement, I encourage you to go for it. The knowledge and qualifications you gain are yours forever, and no one can take that away from you.

* * * * *

There will be struggles that will hit you that you do not deserve, or even see coming. Like sharing a last name with a fictional TV star, and your high school coach, Coach Mennie, randomly yelling, "Hey Punkie Brewster come here!" one day. It's a shame I had to inherit this nickname based on a show that only lasted four seasons. Eventually, I just put "Punkie" on my letter jacket and went on with my life.

But the success story is not overcoming a high school nickname; it's about how life's trajectories can be ironic. Years later, Coach Mennie ended up working for the Sticks while his son was in high school. The tables were turned and I was his "boss," often including "from Punkie" on the memo of his checks. Success is funny like that.

Not all struggles are light-hearted or easily surmountable. It always hurts me when a player leaves the Sticks or an unhappy parent says things about me. It was seven years before we had any real problems in my hometown, but when we did, it left me feeling heartbroken and is something I still struggle with today. The realization that the strong relationships I thought I had with the players' parents could be so fragile and conditional was upsetting. I consider many of our parents to be real, true friends, so it's difficult to realize that some relationships are built on convenience and expectations rather than true friendship. Not all relationships are equal, and some can be more struggle than success.

In retrospect, I realize there have always been unhappy parents in our program; I just may not have been there to witness it. All I can do is take the high road and treat everyone with respect regardless of past interactions. Playing for the Sticks isn't the right place for every player. Ideally, I would love for every player to enjoy and benefit from their time with us. Sadly, that is not the case no matter how much I wish it was.

Players and their families have different perceptions of their summer experience with us. Some players put up huge numbers without receiving a college offer, so their view was that it was not a good summer. Conversely, other players who might not have impressive stats played really well on the right day and got an offer. That player will tell you their time with the Sticks was transformational. Perspective is a hell of a drug.

If there's a success story to be found here, it's that for every player who chooses not to play for Sticks, there are hundreds we have the opportunity to positively impact. We can't dwell on a player who does not want to be a part of the Sticks because we'll lose focus.

It gets tricky when a previously unhappy player wants to come back and play for us as signing day approaches, especially if they haven't received any offers.

The dilemma in this is that it usually wasn't the player's decision to leave. Kids do what their parents tell them to do, and they repeat what mom and dad say behind closed doors. Taking him back will help your program financially and from a talent standpoint. I tend to accept the bulk of the responsibility, thinking, *Well, if we had given him the experience he could not do without, he would still be playing with us.*

The risk of taking the player back is the potential of past issues repeating themselves. Yet, in the end, our primary objective is to aid players in reaching their goal of playing college baseball. Therefore, we often allow them to return, hoping to conclude their journey with us on a positive note, reinforcing the core mission of our program.

I could easily fill this chapter with only the success stories from our journey with the Sticks. But anyone reading this needs to understand the importance of recognizing and expecting failures. Failures are inevitable, and learning from them is vital.

One of the biggest failures occurred in Atlanta, GA, during the summer of 2017. After a game at WWBA, Jaden Hill, Wade Beasley, Alisha, and I stopped by McDonald's. The total came to $4.25, and my company card was declined. A declined transaction of four dollars and twenty-five cents.

Situations like a declined credit card can fracture relationships, partnerships, and friendships. This incident threatened to dismantle one of Arkansas's greatest summer programs before it had a chance to fully flourish. I remember sitting in the car, fighting back tears after the kids had gone back into the hotel.

It would only get worse in the coming days when we did not have enough money in the account to pay our last tournament fee. A parent stepped up and paid the tournament entry fee out of his own pocket. Thankfully, I would repay Johnny Tollett years later after taking over Sticks. The assistance was pivotal – so many positive things have happened since then.

Relationships have played a huge role in our transition from a start-up to realizing the dream phase of owning our own business. As we were headed into our "Hey, we just finished year two, this could be something huge, and not a hobby" phase, we were teetering between potential growth and the brink of collapse. Relationships saved our business before we entered the "Sticks Baseball is not a thing anymore" phase. Without the great relationships with our parents, players, tournament directors, equipment reps, and everyone else we owed money before I took over, there would be no Sticks Baseball today. The relationships you make in your humble beginnings become family during your "championship run" phase. There is no better example than our relationship with Josh Pollack and Derek Hemingway.

In the early days, the Sticks could not get an official apparel contract. We faced issues with high costs and a lack of customization. We were days away from ordering full-price Adidas uniforms in 2018 when we won the Perfect Game MLK Tournament in Phoenix, AZ. Josh Pollack, who was working for 3n2 at the time, called me the next day and offered me everything I had ever wanted. More than a contract, I wanted a partner who believed in the Sticks and was proud to have us represent their brand. Since then, our relationship with Josh and with Derek has been incredibly rewarding. They both attended our wedding, and our bond extends beyond which jersey style we choose each summer.

In April 2023, I took our relationship to the next level by signing a lifetime contract with Decker Sports. I met Tim Decker for the first time at the ABCA Clinic in Nashville, TN, and our subsequent meeting led to this historic partnership. Josh and Derek were already members of the Decker team, so I hated to be the one to break up the band.

Soon after, Alisha and I flew to Omaha, NE, to meet Tim, Derek, Greg Freivogel, and the rest of the Decker team. Josh and Derek have managed our account since our first apparel contract in January 2018, and with this lifetime contract, it seems they will continue to do so indefinitely.

I'm often asked, "When did you know the Sticks made it?" There are many moments but I always think about when we turned down a substantial offer from Nike. They were looking for someone to replace their premier program, but I didn't have the same feeling I had with Josh and Derek, that "this relationship could last forever." Still, it's cool to think about everything Phil Knight has built with Nike, knowing they wanted the Sticks to represent them.

Under Armour (UA) also approached us about becoming one of their top programs for their new baseball division. The excitement of being included in discussions with influential figures in the baseball community was surreal. We met with UA the same day in Nashville at the ABCA about the future of what they were going to do, and they had a great plan. Weeks later, Alisha and I pulled up to the house only for her to say, "What did you order now?" I looked up and saw a huge package on my front door and was very confused. UA had sent me an unexpected care package full of UA items, including two pairs of coaching turfs. To this day, I have no idea how they knew my shoe size or address. Awesome job by Sam to make us feel wanted.

Our uniform journey also includes an intriguing encounter with a rival program's uniform supplier. After a pivotal game at Jupiter during WWBA, I was whisked away in a golf cart for a meeting in a suite at Roger Dean Stadium. I set a condition that for us to join their elite program, they had to drop their current partnership with our instate rivals. They agreed instantly. However, I knew better than to make a decision based on the wrong motives, and the deal eventually fell through.

The struggle to get anyone to believe in us or even consider us a success is something I will never forget. Sharing the stories, including the interest from Nike and others, is surreal and a testament to how far we've come. I encourage you to share your struggles and successes as it will not only inspire others but will remind you of your journey.

Hopefully, our success in the next ten years from now will be tenfold of our past struggles. With our apparel situation secured and a strong partnership with Tim Decker and his team at Decker Sports, we no longer worry about uniform issues. Tim has become a mentor, friend, and business partner, and I'm excited about what the future holds for this relationship.

# Pillar #6

# Treat Your Employees Like Owners

*"No person succeeds alone."*
– Kevin Hart

I've noticed that every coach has a go-to line or phrase, especially during critical moments. Bill Belichick is famous for saying, "Do your job." Simple enough but rarely done effectively. I once worked with Jonathan Gosdin, a great coach who was also known for catchy phrases. During one game, a player counted the number of times Gosdin yelled, "Let's go!" The final number ended up being over 120 times in seven innings.

As coaches, we must remind ourselves to keep things simple amidst chaos, not only for the players but ourselves as well. Over the years with the Sticks, we created so many in-game sayings and vocal cues that Coach Landers labeled them "Brewster-isms." My go-to, and the one that has always made the most sense to me, "Would a good player do that?"

Let's say a player throws his helmet after striking out or backs up the wrong base after a hit because he is not ready mentally. I will say something as simple as, "Would a good player throw his helmet or forget which base to cover?" The answer is always no. I will take it a step further to involve everyday life in the equation. Let's say a player walks past trash in the street. I'll ask,

"Do you think a good player would pick up trash that is not his?" Another popular Brewster-ism is "Do you think a good player would show up five minutes late?"

Hearing it repeatedly has an undeniable effect on the players. There is an immediate embarrassment without embarrassing anyone. They do all the talking by answering the question.

I have kept the same motto and sometimes will simplify it to "Just be a good player" for in-game use. I always want to stay positive and ready for what is next, so when a player makes an error at shortstop, I will say something like, "You will get another ground ball, just be a good player. You are fine." It keeps the same theme of "Would a good player do that?" In this case, a good player missed a ground ball, but it is a positive forward-thinking message to just be a good player on the next one. Even good players make mistakes, but they don't make several in a row. It works well for us, and we can apply it to everyday life.

The essence of this message traces back to a lesson from my dad: "Ask yourself that question out loud," followed by, "You probably know the answer already." This is challenging because, most of the time, the question is something we'd rather avoid. We don't want to pick up someone else's trash or admit that we were late.

Consider a question like, "Should I stay out all night drinking when I have to be at work at 6 am?" When someone asks themselves those questions out loud, they usually know the answer. I encourage you to use these cues and mottos around your workplace, so employees have something quick and simple they can refer to, even when you are not there to guide them. As a business owner, President, or CEO, you can't be present every day. Employees must be comfortable representing the company acting as an extension of you, your values, and your principles.

## Run It Like You Own It

When I hired Evan Hamm as Director of Baseball Operations, his first task was to create the schedule for next year's teams as if he owned the Sticks. He immediately went to ask me a question, and I stopped him by responding with, "I do not answer to anyone as the owner, and right now, neither do you. Make the schedule as if it is 100% your business, and we will compare notes." It was a great exercise for both of us because it confirmed we were on the same page. Fortunately, we only had to change one location.

During Sticks Weekend, we had close to 400 players showing up to kick off summer ball; it was a lot of fun but also very chaotic. Again, I told Evan to run it like he owned it; we would iron out any problems later. Ironically, the first thing out of his mouth was the complete opposite of what I would have done, causing me to stop him before he finished the sentence. I thought it was funny, given the situation, but he was frustrated and worried that I would be mad at him.

I needed to know that he could pull this off without me if I got run over by a bus on the way to the event. The only way to do that is by giving others the freedom to make decisions. My answers and choices are not always right, and my methods are not the only way to get things done, but we won't know for sure until I give others the power to make decisions.

## On-the-Job Training

As a business owner, I provide on-the-job training and hands-on experience anywhere I can. Having benefited from "on-the-job" training early in my career, I know how getting a taste of being in charge and having a voice can change someone's drive and vision.

Cason Tollett has had the best playing career for anyone who played for the Sticks during high school, and he means the world to me. He walked my stepmom down the aisle at our wedding, and his father is our CPA. As a sophomore in high school, Cason chose to attend the University of Arkansas after turning down several other Power 5 schools.

Unfortunately, with the number one catcher in college baseball, Colorado native Casey Opitz, returning for his senior year at Arkansas, it left little room for Cason to be much more than his backup. Arm problems would force Cason to redshirt his freshman year, pushing him further down the depth chart. Then, due to COVID, the MLB reduced its draft from 40 rounds in 2019 to five rounds in 2020 before working its way back to 20 rounds.

With the writing on the wall, it was time for Cason to make some adult decisions about his playing career. He chose to transfer to Arkansas State University and play for legendary coach Tommy Raffo. Cason was finally in charge of the pitching staff and hitting in the middle of the order for the Red Wolves when two concussions in two weeks ended his season. At the time, we were unsure whether it would end his career. Doctors would not clear Cason to play summer baseball, and for the first time in ten years, he had the summer off.

He asked to be an assistant coach on my team, and I have never been more excited to add a coach to our program. He started like everyone else at that stage of their careers—shy and unsure of themselves. He slowly became more vocal in team meetings, and players sought him out for more guidance before and after games. Cason had by far the biggest on-field presence of any Sticks player and carried it over as a de facto team captain. Now as a coach, he was becoming a liaison between the players and coaches, and it was helping me tremendously.

In our third tournament of the year, I saw an opportunity to expand Cason's role. During a game that we won 6-0 after back-to-back walks, I told Cason to do a mound visit with the struggling pitcher and catcher. Visibly surprised, he asked me, "What do I say to them?" As a catcher, Cason had stood in on more mound visits than anyone in the complex. I told him to just say something he remembered from an old mound visit and to have fun. All's well that ends well.

The next week, I let him do the home plate meeting that the head coach normally handles, and he coached first base sometimes as well. He was so happy, and I was so proud. He was asked to be an assistant coach in charge of hitters in the Northwoods Collegiate League for the following summer, which is unheard of for someone his age with no experience. Surprisingly enough, he turned them down to coach with us again. How cool is that?

I challenge you to find ways to help your staff grow and show them what it looks like from the top. I hope nothing more than, one day in the future, to have Evan Hamm as the President of off-the-field operations, Kyle Slayton as President of on-the-field operations, with Cason Tollett following in my footsteps and coaching our top team. Before anyone thinks I am considering retiring, maybe I am just planning for when some MLB team calls me one day. Who knows?

Remember when I said if I get run over by a bus tomorrow, the Sticks must go on? We need a plan in place and a vision for what that looks like. I challenge you to ensure your business will run forever without you, and the guys replacing you know what it looks like to be successful in that position. To make this happen, you must take people along to experience the top seat and allow them to make decisions with you and for you. Give them more responsibility over time, and you trust that they will learn through their mistakes because, let's face it, there will always be mistakes.

While we're talking about the future of my company and what that looks like to me, I challenge you to look at your company now in real time. From the outside looking in, there is one question you must ask yourself: "Would I be a fan of this company if I could select anyone in this space to use as a product or service?" Does your company provide everything on your checklist that would qualify it to be selected for your business or is there someone else in your space who provides what you are looking for as a customer?

It's okay to admit that you would choose someone else; it wouldn't be the end of the world. Some companies have more resources and advantages than others, allowing them to offer different and, at times, better services. You should, however, put in place a plan to move the vision of your company toward what aligns with your checklist. If I'm not the biggest fan of my business, how can I expect anyone else to be?

This exercise of making a checklist of things I would want in a summer baseball program was eye-opening because it told me exactly what I knew. We are doing things at Sticks that I believe in, and that I know will work for years to come. I wrote down five things that I would look for in a summer baseball program if I were a high school player looking for a summer team:

1. Play in the best events possible for my talent level

2. Wear the best uniforms

3. Surround myself with the best group of players and coaches possible to grow as a person over four years together.

4. A program that is most likely to help me get recruited and has a track record to prove they can do it.

5. A program that will allow me to make life-long memories and friends and see places and meet people I never would in high school baseball.

Ironically, all signs point to Sticks Baseball. Maybe that is why we have had success in those departments, because subconsciously we have built it from the heart. Unfortunately, as much as I hate it, we are not for everyone. I wish we were, but we aren't. Maybe a player has "weekly development at a facility each week" on their list. To me, that is separate from summer baseball and is one of the many arguments about our business. Others may want guaranteed innings and playing time, or the least amount of travel possible. Each player's list will be different, that is why it is *their* list. I look forward to you listing five things you would look for when hiring a company in your space and see if they match up with your business outline.

## Treat Everyone Like a Dinner Guest

Somewhere along the way, I heard a saying that really stuck with me and will sum up this entire chapter: "Treat every person you meet like you would a dinner guest." Although I do not remember where I heard it, I do know that it is a very powerful message. I am a huge believer in treating people right. When I think about the act of inviting guests for dinner, there are certain guests you probably invite more often and the conversation flows. Other guests may be more of acquaintances and the conversation or the vibe may be a little "off," but you were still a great host and provided a great evening.

I think back to having a young Cason Tollett and his family for dinner, not knowing that one day he would walk my stepmom down the aisle at our wedding and eventually work for me. Who knows, maybe one day he will run the entire company—all because we treated him well as a dinner guest!

Doing anything great requires time, patience, skill, and most importantly, a ton of luck. My entire career has been the perfect amount of luck, and the blessing of God watching over me. As I get older and explore new hobbies and professions, I often wonder how others did it before me. There's something to be said for being outstanding in one area and below average in nine others rather than being average in ten. It all boils down to how curious you are and how eager you are to step outside the box and attack those items on your dream checklist.

Sometimes, dealing with the parents, the player's attitudes, limited communication from agents, and the constant travel, I often wonder how much easier it would be if I was just an average guy in real estate instead of what I have been labeled great at. Realistically, you would probably be trading one headache for another, because whatever you are passionate about does not stop at 5:00 pm. My mind never stops running around Sticks. I even keep an idea book with me so that I have a place to keep all my thoughts. Sometimes, I am overwhelmed trying to make the Sticks into the best it can be. I know my mind wouldn't work the same way if I were doing something that I was less passionate about.

Ideas come to me from everywhere imaginable, especially social media. A recent tweet by Ben Meer instantly resonated with me, so I knew I had to pass it along in this book. "Make NO your default."

Whether it's new work projects or social gatherings, saying "yes" to non-priorities ruins your priorities. In the words of Mark Manson, "If it is not a F*** yes, then it is a no."

# Pillar #7

# Do One Thing Great and Outsource the Rest

*"People tell us, 'You're really smart.'*
*But no, we just have really smart people around us."*
– Maverick Carter

If you are a business owner or work for a successful company, chances are you're doing one thing really well. You've probably noticed some individuals who are filled with so much creativity and so many ideas that they seem to be leading the pack. The Steve Jobs, Walt Disneys, and Elon Musks of the world are continually reinventing themselves and excelling at everything they do.

For example, Elon Musk has taken all the success he's had with PayPal, SpaceX, and Tesla to transform Twitter into a successful platform. Four different successful companies, in four different markets, all with one thing in common: a successful and creative leader at the top.

Creativity trumps the rest. I often feel that creativity is what sets me apart from my competitors. We always seem to have more innovative ideas and a solid list of backup ideas to pivot to if our original ideas are replicated or the ideas don't work as expected.

If you ask someone what I do best, the answer will be recruiting. That has always been my superpower, and I would be lying if I said I was not good at it. I feel like it is easy to recruit players because of all the tools the Sticks offer and our out-of-the-box thinking.

# Get Creative

### Uniforms/Gear

Creatively, we changed the landscape of summer ball in the Midwest by wearing colored pants before other teams. The navy and red pants were a hit from the very beginning, as were some of our clothing designs that sold out when we made them available, like the "Home of Arkansas Baseball" fall workout shirt we offered a few years ago.

We provide our players with more gear than any other program because we want them to wear it all the time—to school, practice, Perfect Game events, you name it—we want our guys wearing Sticks gear. Our creative apparel designs make our players walking billboards. We have partnered with Decker Sports, which I believe is the best company for custom apparel for high school athletes. They make our ideas and designs come to life through their work.

### Schedule

Traveling for baseball is not easy and can be expensive. Playing locally saves time and money and offers you a better chance to win geographically. Our idea was to change that. My dream was to use baseball as a way to see the world, and we've done just that. How and where we travel to play baseball has been an adventure.

From cars and buses to private jets, we've played in locations like Las Vegas, NV, Phoenix, AZ, Anaheim, CA, Cary, NC, Cedar Rapids, IA, Atlanta, GA, Fort Myers, FL, West Palm Beach, FL, New York, NY, Chicago, IL, and everywhere in between.

In 2022, we were invited to play in Barcelona, Spain in the Perfect Game International Tournament, but the dates conflicted with Jupiter and Fort Myers, making Spain impossible to pull off. Before we started the Sticks, we took a group of 18 players, three coaches, and about 30 parents to play in Alaska for ten days in 2013.

We took our crazy and creative ideas and used the best tournament services nationally in Perfect Game and PBR, as well as 2D Sports regionally, and traveled anywhere and everywhere to play. Crafting a schedule with such extensive travel year after year requires imagination and innovative thinking.

**Social Media Graphics**

Usually, when a player commits to a college, his summer program will post a picture of him on their social media accounts with a caption that says "Congratulations!" A decade ago, it wasn't common for a summer program to post a graphic for every player who committed to playing college baseball or got drafted, but that is exactly what The Sticks did.

We were also one of the first programs to use lineup graphics for every game and share them on social media with a different theme each week. After each game, we follow up with a post, win or lose, and share some stats after every game. I knew every time that we did this, the post would get retweeted and shared by everyone tagged. Also, college and professional scouts could quickly see who was playing and pitching each game. The Sticks is fortunate to have Blaine Tanner, one of the most talented souls who ever worked for us. Blaine played at Morehead State, studied graphic design, and became a force on social media for us.

## Media

Along with Blaine Tanner, Black Cobra Media & Texarkana GameDay have taken our pictures, audio, and video to another level. If I have an idea, they can pull it off flawlessly. It might involve having me mic'd up during a pitching change, talking to Ethan Long about the home run he was about to hit, and telling him to "Pick a house out there and hit it." Or the ideas that Morgan Smith, Nick Reed, and others have that help the Sticks pre- and post-game with interviews, hype/build-up videos, and keeping everyone up to date on which local players have offers from which schools.

Willie Prince, owner of Black Cobra Media, has turned every idea we have ever had into a masterpiece. These guys truly are the best at what they do, and I am so thankful for them. We also have extended our media ideas to other avenues, such as starting our player's podcast, "Why Play Anywhere Else" and my personal podcast, "The Chase Brewster Show."

Jayce Ridling has flawlessly executed our ideas for the "Why Play Anywhere Else" Podcast. With zero training and no idea what I was doing, the first season of "The Chase Brewster Show" saw all nine episodes receive over one thousand views. The Why Play Anywhere Else" Podcast is recorded every Tuesday and Thursday as Jayce hosts three Sticks players on each show. We noticed on some other podcasts that the same players were being interviewed repeatedly, and we wanted every Sticks player to experience what it is like to be interviewed. So far, it has been a wonderful experience for the players and their families.

We have several feature-length videos for the Sticks, and for Summer 2024, we are in the process of putting together an eight-part documentary series for our White Sox Scout Team to premiere each week.

This book falls under that category of *ideas I think are great and hope our players and parents also love.* Anything we can do to highlight the Sticks, whether through audio, video, or text, benefits our brand and our players.

## Network

Luckily, one thing I do great is maintain an extensive network that will hopefully help keep the Sticks at the top for a long time. Our network of people who do great things at Sticks Baseball has been an unbelievable resource for us. For the things we are not great at doing, we have been able to hire people who are. Having the best people in their field working together on projects has helped keep us at the top for a long time.

Our business model is similar. We are one of few programs in the country whose founder does not earn one cent off the youth organizations that feed into our high school program. We have partnerships with some of the greatest youth baseball organizations because we don't tell them how to run their programs, how much to charge, or what players should be on what team. In return, they do not tell us how to run the high school program. Not only is it a great business solution, but we also get to work with some of the greatest people in the region.

Shane Halter, who played in the MLB for ten years, runs our program in Texarkana, TX/AR. Cory Lambert, who pitched at Arkansas State University, runs our youth programs at Max Velocity in Jonesboro, AR. Former Arkansas Razorback star Matt Vinson with Legacy Sports in Northwest Arkansas takes care of all our players in the Fayetteville, AR area. Former college All-American and college coach Cesar Abreu runs our Sticks youth program in Russellville, AR, out of Abreu Baseball Academy. Former Division One coach Jon Tatum and Jeremy Myers run the Central Arkansas youth Sticks program out of Benton, AR, at his Spartan Academy. They are six of the brightest and best coaches the state has to offer.

This arrangement allows our players to train freely. It has been a true blessing for us to grow our network and find great people to run something that we are not great at—the youth programs for the Sticks. We can focus on what we do great–the high school side–and the results have been amazing.

## What are You Great at?

I think it is important to look in the mirror and ask, "What am I great at?" Not pretty good, or what you enjoy doing, but what is the one thing you are truly great at doing? Can you pinpoint this talent, and do you have the data to support your realization? Maybe you are in sales, and the data is in black and white from your first major account. Maybe you are a coach with an impeccable win-loss record and dozens of championship trophies sitting behind your desk. More importantly, do you know off the top of your head what you need to outsource to others without thinking? Sometimes, it is much harder to admit what we do not do well than recognize what we do well.

It's important to look at your team and your circle and see what they do great around you. Ideally, you should be able to identify these strengths effortlessly. Everyone close to you must bring something unique to the table that helps you or your business. Just one thing! They may be great at running your errands and running your life and business smoothly. Maybe they are the smartest person in the room or someone you cannot run your business without. Each person in your circle must bring a distinct, exceptional skill to the table. Relying solely on networking to compensate for your team's flaws isn't a sustainable strategy for success.

## Other Professionals (CPA, Lawyer, etc.)

While we are on the subject of outsourcing help, I highly recommend you find a great CPA. Growing up, I had no idea what a CPA did or what a tax write-off was. Johnny Tollett not only provided me with a player who has had the best career of any Sticks player, but he also has become a mentor to me and has given me some of the best tax advice I could ever ask for. You do not need an H&R Block app to handle your taxes. You need someone you trust wholeheartedly who is a text message away to answer any questions you may have. Unfortunately, my CPA is not taking any new clients, so you will have to find someone else.

I also recommend having a good lawyer in your network. I have been so blessed to work with two of the best people from my hometown, Kyle Davis, and Olivia Shepard. I cannot overstate how wonderful they were to me and my family. Luckily for me, knock on wood, we have not needed them for any major legal issues yet. It has primarily been petty paperwork stuff, especially waivers during COVID-19. My approach to everything was to make sure I had great relationships with people I trusted so that if something significant ever came up, I wouldn't have to argue about billable hours or whose case was a priority. I needed to know that if I have a life-or-death situation, there is someone involved who I know will wholeheartedly defend me and fight for me. If those two ever happen to read this, I love you both and cannot thank you enough for putting up with me and all my phone calls over the years.

I cannot close this chapter without mentioning several people in my life who have made my life easier. As you might have noticed, I value relationships with those deeply invested in my family and me whom I trust implicitly. I cannot stress the importance of this enough. While you may not currently require everything I've mentioned, make sure you can trust those in your network.

I will never have to worry that my financial advisor is robbing me blind. Mike Cobb has been heaven-sent, and I cannot thank him enough for taking me on as a client when I had basically zero money. He has set up our retirement and helped us build a long-term plan for my family and me. Mike has been a tremendous mentor to me as well. His son, Jackson, is one of the best players who has played for us and is currently starting in the infield for University of Kansas. Mike's dad, Jimmy Cobb, is eighty-plus years old and still gets up and goes to work every day. If you are going to get a financial advisor, I recommend getting one who has a bloodline and a vision of still doing it when he is 80.

I also have the greatest home builder you can ask for in Kevin Browning and his wife Christal. Alisha and I built during the middle of COVID-19 when supplies were hard to find and extremely overpriced. Everyone around us, without ever asking for more details, would tell us how we were getting ripped off and that everything was priced too high. I never once listened to those comments or questioned Kevin, and never would. He and his wife have become family to us, and they will build every house we ever live in. Their oldest son Spencer was our first eighth grader to commit to play college baseball, committing to the University of Arkansas. He is the greatest kid ever and has so much pressure on him that it is almost a shame to allow players to commit at such a young age. I always tell him, though, "Better to be in this position than to be someone no one wants." Time will tell, but the promise is there for him to be one of the next great players to come out of Texarkana.

Purchasing a home or car is among the most significant and stressful adult decisions. Browning Homes has us covered on the house side of things, and Steve Landers, and his right-hand man, Brett Huskey, have taken care of our automotive needs. I highly recommend having a trusted individual in your network for car purchases to avoid the unpredictability of random car lot shopping. Find someone like I have in Steve or Brett who can order any car I want at any time. They already know my budget, my story, and my preferences. It is a much easier process, and easier is better.

Brett's son Jordan is one of the best left-handed pitchers we have had come through the Sticks program and is currently playing at Florida Southwestern JUCO, after transferring from the University of Arkansas. Every start Jordan made with us over the years, Tripp Landers caught him. Tripp, an outstanding defensive catcher who hits left-handed, recently transferred from TCU to Florida Southwestern with Jordan. It's kind of cool to see their parents, who are best friends and work together on everything, have their kids follow their dreams simultaneously 45 minutes away from them. Full circle moment.

## Network Circles (Like Mentor Circles)

Again, I cannot stress to you enough the importance of keeping a good network, both within your business among employees and in your personal life. Being an adult is hard, and determining whom to trust at times is a nightmare. We all need good people in our circle who help us make adult decisions, both personally and professionally. My network has naturally centered around baseball. I believe we have been good to our players, and the parents think we have been good to their kids. This has enabled us to build relationships with parents through baseball. Again, how cool is that?

I could mention so many more people, like Garrett Huff, who was our star shortstop on our State Championship team at Genoa Central. Garret now handles everything in my personal account at the bank for me. Frank Halter and Billy Lavender, whose sons played a huge role in the Sticks, are also my go-to for banking help. Billy's very talented son Trey Lavendar played with us before signing to play with Cameron University. Billy was the mastermind who helped bring Southern Athletics and Sticks Baseball together.

Several years before, I had passed on going to work for Frank and Shane Halter at Southern Athletics, something I did not want to do because of our relationship and because Texarkana meant so much to me. Deep down, I wanted something so much bigger than something local or even regional, and I knew that to make what I wanted for my career, I needed to branch out. Unfortunately, this strained my relationship with two people I love for a while, but Billy mended those fences, and we have done great things ever since. Frank has blessed our program with three great players of his own: Jackson, who is currently a junior at the University of Louisiana Lafayette; Jarret, who has several offers and just came off a great sophomore campaign at Pleasant Grove; and Judson, one of the best middle school players in East Texas. Frank, Shane, and Billy all hold a special place in my heart.

I won't list every single person who has ever helped me, but I need to emphasize that how you treat people, and in my case, how you treat their sons, will provide you with long-lasting friendships and help expand your network. These friendships have helped turn my network into something special, and I am forever thankful for everyone inside my circle of trust.

Seek out trustworthy and valued individuals to include in your network. You should find the most qualified people for specific roles or develop a team of trusted loved ones into top performers. Your network is an extension of you, so enhance its value as much as you can because it will, in return, add value to you.

# Pillar #8

# Be a Dreamer and Believe in Yourself

*"You cannot share your dream and vision with everyone."*
– Steve Harvey

The most important line in this book: **You must be a dreamer, and you must believe in yourself.** Everything else you can teach yourself or hire someone to do it for you. My story is the perfect example. I did not play baseball growing up; I was a team manager in high school, and now I am one of the top coaches in my profession. That is the definition of being a dreamer, believing in yourself, and God's plan working overtime for you.

At the time of writing, my Instagram bio for @Brewsterc29 reads **A Dreamer * Son * Brother * Husband * Business Owner * Head Coach of Sticks Baseball/White Sox Scout Team * Host of The Chase Brewster Show.**

Your social media bio is your virtual first impression, so the first item listed in my Instagram bio is important to me: *A Dreamer*.

## Dreams

Being a dreamer is something I deeply believe in. A child will tell their parents at a young age that they want to be an astronaut or a doctor when they grow up. Mom or dad will listen to their children and tell them they can be anything they want to be.

As we get older, though, somewhere along the way, others seem to decide for us what is realistic and what is not. "You will never get into this school," or "You will never play in the NFL." I don't understand why this is. Today, we have more resources and knowledge to help us do anything we want to do in life. We can see things that are attainable and touch them. We can fall in love with subjects and concepts and develop a passion for doing something great, like curing cancer because a family member died from the horrible disease.

Maybe someone wants to pass the bar and work on domestic violence or child custody cases because of some bad experiences in their own life. Yet, some non-believers with no dreams will tell you that living out your dreams is impossible.

Let me tell you, anything is possible. Some dreams require more work and skills than others. Playing in the NFL at 5'7" is a tall task, but it has been done. Now is the time to put your dreams for your business front and center. Whatever you are dreaming is not big enough.

## Personal Goals

When it comes to your personal goals, dream even bigger. If I can publish a book and have a podcast, think of what you can do. Some other options for the title of this book were "No One is Going to Read That" (the podcast would be called "No One is Going to Watch That"), "A Dreamer," and "You Can Change the World" before we eventually picked "Why Play Anywhere Else: How We Built Sticks Baseball into a National Brand."

We primarily chose this title because I knew we could change the world together if I could share my story. I also wanted to make sure the Sticks got the credit it deserved in the title, so it was very conflicting. The notebook in which I wrote this entire project has "You Can CTW Part 1" handwritten in black Sharpie.

Dreaming requires having a non-stop imagination. The Sticks Fall League is our most significant creation to date. The idea came to me one day while I was in the shower, daydreaming about what the league's future could be one day. We had traveled to Shreveport the weekend before for a tournament. Going into the tournament, our fall record was 16-0; this was our last tournament. It was a two-day tournament, meaning we would have to stay the night.

Our team was an 18U team, made up of mostly seniors, and we were extremely talented. PJ Hilson, who would sign with the University of Alabama and eventually get drafted by the San Francisco Giants later that year in the 7th round, was hitting leadoff. University of Arkansas signee Nick Griffin hit in the two-hole and played RF next to Hilson, who was in CF. University of Arkansas signee Trey Harris played LF to round out the unbelievable outfield.

We were very talented offensively and led on the mound by University of Arkansas left-hander Zack Morris and Ole Miss signee Kaleb Hill, who would go on to get drafted by the St. Louis Cardinals later that year. Chris Williard, who would start at Ouachita Baptist University as a freshman in their infield was also on this team. I will tell you all of this to explain the context of what kind of team traveled all that way to compete.

At the home plate meeting for Game One, the head coach for the opposing team was former Cy Young winner and Milwaukee Brewers ace Ben Sheets. He started the meeting by saying "Hey Chase, take it easy on us. These guys are all fifteen years old." I was shocked. This was an 18U tournament that we had to travel to play in, and we were opening the tournament against a group that had not yet played a game of high school baseball. It was not ideal. We scored seven runs in the first inning and between innings, I asked the tournament director what was going on. His response was "We did not have enough 18U teams to fill the tournament, and I knew if I told you that you were going to have to play against 15- and 16-year-olds in pool play, you would not have come." He was right.

We made the most of a tough situation and had a great weekend. Not every team was younger than us, and we had some challenges. In the final game against a strong DBAT team, we went down 10-0 in the first inning and came back to win the game and the championship 12-10 thanks to an incredible pitching performance by Jackson Huskey. We finished the fall 21-0 and had a great time. Why wouldn't we? Winning is fun.

After we returned home, all I could think about was our team and the competition we had faced that fall. 21-0 was impressive, and even more so considering the year before, we went 10-0 in the fall playing doubleheaders at colleges. 31-0 in two years. I knew something had to change. The travel was not fun, and the competition was not always ideal. The worst part as a business owner was that I could not control any of it. All I could do was pay the tournament fees and hope for the best.

If a starting pitcher struggled to get out of the first inning, it would throw everything into a funk for the entire weekend. The fall normally sees smaller rosters, and a byproduct of that is a smaller pitching staff. Because of pitch count rules, one bad inning from a pitcher could leave a position player who does not pitch often on the mound. Luckily for us, so far, we had better players than everyone else, and our coaching staff did not mess things up. Something had to change for us to reach our potential as a program to get the most out of the fall for our players.

I knew we had to do something where I could control the amount of travel, the competition, the venue, the time slots, and the prime matchups so college coaches would know when and where to watch. I just wasn't sure exactly how to do it.

## Practice

The two main purposes for playing fall ball are to get players ready to play for their high school seasons in the spring and to get recruited. So, I focused on these two things as I built out my master plan.

First, I had to secure dates at top colleges before other tournament directors booked them. In March, I started reaching out to everyone in my network of college coaches to book fields six months in advance. We scheduled our Fall League workout for colleges to watch the players work out on September 1, 2018, at Henderson State University, a beautiful all-turf Division 2 school in Arkadelphia, AR.

The next day, the coaches get together for the first-ever Sticks Fall League Player Draft. Coaches would draw numbers out of a hat and draft players on a whiteboard at Flying Burger, a local restaurant. After lunch, with the draft selection finally over, the dream was now becoming a reality as the first year of the Sticks Fall League was underway.

We were set to play at several in-state colleges, such as Hendrix University, Southern Arkansas, and Arkansas Tech. Like most startups or dreams, not everyone saw the vision in our dreams in the beginning, leaving us to play mostly at the Division 2 schools in the state. These are beautiful stadiums, but outside of Henderson State, they were all grass fields. Each week, when it rained, it felt like months of dreaming and planning were for nothing. Literally. We would have to get creative, but we managed to get every game in. We had six teams that first year: Sticks Red, Green, Yellow, Orange, White, and Grey. We kept standings like a high school conference would, and we also built the rosters just like a high school team would. Teams consisted of incoming freshmen, sophomores, juniors, and seniors. The matchups were fun and intense, but most importantly, people love something new.

We rewarded the players with Player of the Week, Pitcher of the Week, and Freshman of the Week. We also had an All-Star Game on a Wednesday night halfway through the season, with recruiters from almost every college in Arkansas, both the D1 and D2, as well as several out-of-state colleges in attendance. It was the biggest non-PBR event in the state since we started. Genoa Central's Cason Brigham took home the MVP honors that night, hitting a double and throwing two scoreless innings. As we closed out the fall, just like we drew it up, the last-place Sticks Red team won three straight games in the playoffs to win the Sticks Fall League Championship. Pottsville senior Mason Huie won the Playoff Game MVP and the Sticks Fall League Player of the Year award and committed to play baseball at Southern Arkansas University during his historic run. It was so fun to watch.

In the five-plus years since we started the Sticks Fall League, we grew from six teams to as many as 21 teams. We had to use colors like Sticks Teal or Pink, and even different shades of Green. We have had so many great performers and memorable players. There may not be a bigger story than left-handed pitcher Hayden Hable in the fall of 2020. Hayden was the first player from Louisiana to play in our Fall League. He played for Sticks White, which despite having two extremely talented arms, was what most would say was a subpar team. His Sticks White teammate Northwestern State commit Grayson Gates won the semifinal game, setting the stage for Hayden Hable to keep his storybook season alive and did he ever. He went seven innings with twelve strikeouts and won the Playoff MVP Award. It is important to note that this was all during COVID. In-person recruiting was non-existent during this time. Justin Pettigrew, head baseball coach at SAU, was the only college coach to come watch a Sticks Fall League game the entire fall. He saw Hayden that day and eventually would sign him to SAU. In Hayden's freshman year, SAU would spend time at Number One in the country in the rankings, and eventually play in the D2 World Series. Hard work pays off, in this case, for both Hayden and for Coach Pettigrew.

We were able to control everything in the Fall League because it was all Sticks teams. This allowed us to change the rules to ensure our players were as successful as possible. If you have a summer program, I highly recommend using some of the following rules.

## Runs per Inning

A maximum of five runs could be scored per inning until the last inning. Once a team scored more than five runs in an inning, we automatically changed out the teams in the field. One negative aspect of this rule was that if, for example, a team had already scored four runs in an inning, and then a player hit a three-run home run, only one would count. This would help us save on pitching, making sure that every team had the guys lined up to throw their pitch count each weekend. The only exception to this rule is in the 9th inning, there are no restrictions on the number of runs a team can score.

## Pitch Counts

Each hitter starts his at-bat with a 1-1 count. Pitchers love this; hitters hate it. I got this idea at a Razorback Camp when Razorback Pitching Coach Wes Johnson and Head Coach Dave Van Horn invited me to watch some of our younger players participate. During a scrimmage, they started every batter with a 1-1 count. It was a fantastic idea that enabled good pitchers to possibly throw all nine innings while keeping their pitch count low. To prevent injuries from overuse, we had a max pitch count of 65 in the first year. We have changed that number from year to year, as there does not seem to be a perfect situation. One year, it seems too low, but the next year when everyone is throwing complete games in 80 pitches, it tells us that it might be too high. We have yet to find a perfect number, but each year we get more data to make it as close to perfect as we can.

## Extra Innings

The most controversial rule is by far our extra inning rule: Bases loaded, two outs, 3-2 count. One year, Sticks Columbia lost 1-0 in the semi-finals of the playoffs on this rule, and I hated it for the players. The pitcher threw one pitch, a ball, to end the game at 1-0. Many parents do not realize that we have agreements with schools on what hours we can be on the field, and most will not allow us to use their lights. We must do everything we can to find a winner on the field, and this rule does that. We have since changed the rule to one out, with each batter starting in a 3-2 count. Again, the idea is to find a winner.

The Sticks Fall League has by far been our biggest success story of being a dreamer and believing that we could pull it off. No matter what industry you're in, I promise you that believing in your crazy ideas will be worth it. Your success will make others wonder why they didn't think of it themselves. Since the start of the Sticks Fall League, other programs in the state have tried to start their own Fall Leagues. They cannot get enough players, or the caliber of talent the players in our league have, so they use a pitching machine with the message that it is to help save pitchers' arms. Who really knows if they believe in protecting arms, or if they simply do not have arms to play 18-inning games? Their problems are not my problems, thankfully. We are excited about the changes and additions we are making this fall to hopefully make our sixth year the best year.

## Sticks Hall of Fame

As a way to say *Thank You*, we started the Sticks Hall of Fame (HOF). Perhaps some players appreciate the gesture more than others, but we see how much it means to the families of the players selected.

The HOF was initiated in 2018 during our College Signee Dinner. This event honored every senior who signed to play college baseball. University of Arkansas assistant coach Nate Thompson spoke at our banquet. The inaugural class inducted infielder Gionti Turner and Coach Tommy Richardson. Turner, a Watson Chapel High School graduate who had signed with Three

Rivers Community College before being selected in the 27th round of the 2018 MLB Draft by the Cleveland Indians. Coach Richardson was instrumental in starting the Sticks program and was a member of our original coaching staff. His eldest son, Jacob, has significantly contributed to our coaching staff, and his youngest son, Will, was a key player for us and has since become one of our top coaches.

In 2019, the HOF inducted Nettleton High School's star outfielder, PJ Hilson, a sixth-round draft pick by the San Francisco Giants, and Mason Philley, a left-handed pitcher from the University of Arkansas – Monticello. Unfortunately, this was our final year to have the banquet due to the COVID-19 pandemic in 2020. UALR head coach Chris Curry did a phenomenal job speaking at our last event.

We eventually adjusted the selection process for the HOF players and began announcing our selections during our Sticks Weekend event at the start of the summer. The 2021 inductees included Horatio High School's right-handed pitcher Wade Beasley, drafted by the Milwaukee Brewers, and CJ Harris, who tragically passed away at such an early age.

The 2022 HOF inductees would be our largest and most talented class to date, including second-round picks Masyn Winn (Cardinals), Jaden Hill (Rockies), Tink Hence (Cardinals), and fourteenth-rounder Braylon Bishop (Pirates). In 2023, we welcomed ninth-rounder Connor Noland (Cubs), former Phillies minor leaguer Matt Goodheart, Arkansas–Pine Bluff standout outfielder Ja'Kobi Jackson, and Sticks founder and coach Steve Landers, Jr.

I am proud to announce that Richardson, Beasley, and Goodheart have transitioned to coaching roles with the Sticks after their playing days. Other former players, like Matt Akin and Preston Pope, have also joined our coaching staff.

I cannot officially comment on the 2024 Sticks Hall of Fame class; however, I know that Cason Tollett, Peyton Holt, Josh Hyneman, and Aiden Adams all deserve to have their names called at some point soon, given their significant contributions to the Sticks. We hope this honor will be a source of enduring pride for players, allowing them to reflect fondly on their experiences and the love of the game for years to come.

We are asked often if there are enough players to continue to announce players every year. We still have not inducted two big leaguers, Logan O'Hoppe and Jonathan Ornelas, so I think we will have candidates for a while.

## My Dreams

It would be impossible to talk about being a dreamer and believing in yourself without mentioning the example you are holding in your hands. This book has been my biggest dream and the most difficult thing to keep belief in my entire career. So many times, I would think *nobody is going to read this, I am not a writer,* or *I would embarrass myself.* If you truly believe you can change the world, you will move past these fears. Something like writing a book is so minute in changing the world, but hopefully, this book will help that process.

I am a very confident person, and I believe in myself wholeheartedly. I know that I have some of the craziest ideas that you could think of. I am still a little embarrassed at how secretive I was while writing this book. I was already insecure about the project, and I knew if I told the wrong person and word got out before it was published, I would change my mind, not the world. I didn't announce it to the world until I knew that I was close enough to completing this project that nothing would stop me from going to press. That is what really separated me from being the dreamer I am now, even when I thought I was dreaming big.

I knew subconsciously that I would do this for myself and for anyone who believed in me. It was like a sixth sense that for my dream to shine bright, I had to hold my cards as long as possible. I knew that by the time this book came out, we would do such a good job with the press and the roll out of the telling of our story and our mission that there would be so much excitement, making everyone want to read my story. I dream that one day, someone will talk about this book and how easy it was for me to write and publish this project so that they can write their own book. If you are reading it. If you have dreams of telling your story, I challenge you to get started today. I bought a $6.99 journal at Books-A-Million and started writing. I encourage you to do the same.

I can also tell you that when we announced that my podcast, *The Chase Brewster Show*, was coming out, we had not yet recorded one episode. After all the years of talking myself out of it, I finally told myself if I just put the announcement out, I would be forced to figure it out. I had the budget to get all the software and equipment. I knew the people, and I knew I was semi-charming enough to make each episode work, I just had to figure it out in due time. No matter when I started, I knew that my first episode would not be as good as my 50th or even 100th episode. I know right now that my second book will be better than this one. Yes, I am enough of a dreamer that I have other books in the works in my mind. I challenge you right now, just start! Whatever it is that you are dreaming about, start it today. It will be the best feeling of your career, I promise you. Do not let an occupation define you. Being a baseball coach by trade doesn't exclude me from getting involved in real estate, a podcast, or writing a book. If you can dream about it, you can do it. If you believe in yourself and can prove to the world your talent and worth, they will pretend that they always believed in you from the start.

Jalen Hurts is an excellent example of this. Jalen was an unbelievably talented quarterback coming out of high school in Texas, signing with the University of Alabama to play football. Jalen would go on to be the first freshman ever to start at quarterback for Nick Saban. After leading his team to the National Championship Game in 2016, although he did not play his best, Jalen would take them back to the National Championship Game in 2017. After halftime of the game against Georgia, Saban would go with freshman Tua Tagovailoa to start the third quarter, who would lead the team to a come-from-behind victory to win the National Championship. All the good that Jalen had done in Tuscaloosa was forgotten. The next year, his junior season, he split time with Tagovailoa. After the 2018 season, Jalen transferred to the University of Oklahoma, finishing his college career as the runner-up for the Heisman while leading the Sooners to the College Football Playoffs. Jalen was a dreamer who believed in himself even when many in the sports world did not.

He would go on to play in the Super Bowl for the Eagles and finish as runner-up for the MVP in 2022. As Hurts continued to receive accolades and awards in the NFL, social media erupted as Alabama claimed him as an alumnus. Suddenly, they wanted to claim the player that they no longer wanted once he was on top in the NFL. Jalen took the high road like he always does, but there is still some irony in the post.

# Pillar #9

# Embrace What Scares You

*"Just because it hasn't been done before,*
*doesn't mean you shouldn't try it."*
– Howard Schultz

Do you remember earlier when I said I was terrified to fly? One September, I booked a flight to Phoenix, AZ, to attend a tournament that was scheduled for the following January. The next three nights, I had night terrors. On the fourth day, I canceled my flight, and I slept that entire night without waking up once. Eventually, I realized flying was not bad; worrying about the worst-case scenario is what scares you. In the end, how awesome is it to be 30,000 feet in the air and see everything God has blessed us with?

Alisha and I were given tickets to the Rawlings Gold Glove Dinner in New York City. This invite-only suit and tie event is the biggest baseball banquet of the year. There was no way I could back out. The entire flight from Dallas to New York, I repeated to myself, "You asked for this life. You cannot do things like this without flying."

We had a great time with Steve Cohen, Steve Napolitano, Shaun Manning, and everyone else associated with Rawlings. I also proposed to Alisha that weekend.

Two things that scare me the most are death and working for someone else. Unfortunately, I cannot control death. I have, however, started working out and eating better and have lost over 85 pounds. I'm doing all I can on my end to live longer, but I'm not 100% in control of my fate.

I can, however, control not having to work for someone else. I worked for a school district for seven years doing 7:30 AM bus duty. Because I had a thirty-minute drive to work, I was up at 5:45 AM every day to get there on time. I absolutely loved my time at Genoa Central and working for Debbie Huff. I also hope to never work for another high school.

There are 24 hours in a day. Most people work for eight hours and probably sleep for another eight hours, leaving eight hours to enjoy the day. What about the time it takes for you to shower and get ready for your day? Or the time it takes to travel to and from work? The minutes available for you are disappearing quickly.

I enjoy waking up at 10:00 AM (11 if I'm lucky), getting a quick workout in, and finding lunch before it's time to nap. Then, I'm up until midnight or 1:00 AM working. I have no choice but to make all the right moves and hire a great team around me because I never want to go back to work at 7:30 AM. Knock on wood.

This mindset drives every move I make. There has to be more to life than spending most of your day working for someone else. If you are considering working for yourself, I encourage you to start today. It may not be easy, and you likely will not have all the answers, but you will figure it out.

For many years, Alisha worked at the same daycare. Eventually, the daycare moved its entire staff to run an all-day preschool at an elementary school. She would leave the house every day by 6 AM and often not return home until after 5:30 PM. She is a very caring, loving, and beautiful soul who loves children and people. So, I do not doubt that she was great at her job. She worked year-round and had only attended a handful of Sticks games since we started the program. COVID allowed her to make every single Sticks game during the summer of 2020, and we were extremely talented, so it made for a great time.

Due to COVID-19 guidelines, we had to travel out of state all summer. The Sticks were having a winning season, and Alisha and I had a lot of fun together. When she went back to work, it was miserable. She was up at 5 AM, meaning I was up at 5 AM, too, and always went to bed early because she had to be up so early. The hours started to weigh on our marriage. We were not wealthy by any means, and I know it's common for both people in the marriage to work. But also, in the back of my mind, I knew I would need to work harder than ever to cover her salary so she could quit, and that is exactly what I did.

Alisha became such a huge part of Sticks and Sticks Weekend, which is our opening weekend event of the summer. We could not have pulled off Sticks Weekend as we grew without her. As Sticks Weekend was approaching and everything was lining up for 2021 to be our biggest summer ever, she came to me with bad news.

The first Friday of Sticks Weekend that year was Friday, May 27, my birthday. We would have to spend my birthday weekend in Little Rock, working Sticks Weekend. It turned out that the school denied her request for the day off because she was not allowed to miss the last day of school. My biggest fear was coming true—Alisha had a boss who was affecting her life. I told Alisha that I had been working hard all year to save money so she could quit her job and spend every second with me, the dogs, and the Sticks. At first, she did not want to retire early, but now she will tell you that her biggest fear is working for someone else.

My dad and I could not be more different. He will tell you his biggest fear is his boss thinks someone else could do his job better or the company no longer needs him or his position. He has told me a million times that he gets up and goes to work, even when he is sick, so no one could ever think he was replaceable.

Immediately after my dad's birth in 1960, a priest was called to pray over him because the doctors did not think he would make it. A visiting surgeon felt like he could save him. At three days old, my dad was split open for six-plus hours. He has had health problems all his life, mostly stomach-related. In 2015, he had a quadruple bypass, followed by having part of his colon removed, and his gallbladder taken out. Throughout all of this, the only thing on his mind was getting back to work to keep his job.

After several years of begging, in June 2023, I finally talked him into retiring and coming to work for us as our personal assistant. We celebrated by having him and my stepmom attend the PBR Showdown at Lakepoint in Atlanta, GA, to watch the Sticks start our summer off. We would have five teams playing in Atlanta at once, so it would be a great weekend to attend. This would be the first time he would watch the Sticks play in person since we started the program. I will never forget the joy of my dad getting to watch me coach the Sticks for the first time and see what it has become after watching us start this from the ground up.

The Sticks went 24-4 as an organization that weekend. Our 15U and 16U teams won the tournament in their age group, and our 17U team that I coach finished 5-1 on the weekend, losing in the Championship to another nationally ranked team. It was a fantastic weekend and an absolute joy to experience with my dad, stepmom, and Alisha.

He has already been an enormous help to us. On his first day on the job, he went through the "junk mail" and found a $1500 refund check from our insurance company. I trust him with our personal account information and never worry about missing money or jobs not getting done. More importantly, I go to bed every night, knowing he does not have to get up early the next day for work.

My biggest accomplishment in my career has been helping Alisha and my dad both leave their jobs. In December of 2023, we learned that my dad had lung cancer. Since getting that awful news, he has rarely been able to get out of bed while doctors are figuring out his treatment options. If he was still employed by someone else, he would not be able to go to work every day and would be unable to pay his bills for his family. I cannot thank God enough for putting me in a position to provide for the people I love after they have done so much for me.

I tell these stories to be as honest as possible with you, and let you know that everyone's biggest fears are just that—theirs! I could not make him stop working, and he could not make me apply for the next high school job that came open. I have learned and invested time in real estate and other business opportunities to make sure I can wake up whenever I want to, and so that my wife does not have to ask for time off to travel the world with me. How can we change the world if we spend 16 of our 24 hours every day sleeping and working?

## Financial Freedom

The biggest life hack there is having financial freedom. It is not lost on me that everyone in the world would love to sleep in, make a ton of money, and travel the world. I am not some out-of-touch millionaire telling you some random advice that will never work. I am telling you that if it scares me enough to have to be at work at 7:30 AM every morning, years and years of planning and working extremely hard was all to be able to eventually set my hours and schedule. I still work hard, every day. My time is more valuable than ever now, and I am now doing things that I never dreamed of. From writing this book to working on my very successful podcast "The Chase Brewster Show" or working on other new content, there never seems to be a slow moment.

Today I was asked to record an interview next Tuesday with Earl Gill and Tyler Houff for their podcast "The Power Hour" which also airs on our local radio station. Yesterday I was asked by my good friend Morgan Smith who owns Texarkana Gameday to come to their live show "The Drop" next Wednesday with him, Nick Reed, Zach Doty, and Cameron Sullivan. I must submit the article I was asked to write for Texarkana Magazine by next Friday. I also must be up early Friday for our weekly Zoom Decker Leadership Meeting with the entire Decker crew to make sure everything is good and up to date for all our players. Keep in mind that this is on top of my full-time job as President of Sticks

Baseball and as President of our new startup company Brewster Inc. Lucky for me, I get to set my own hours to get everything done.

When you love what you do, it never feels like work. I challenge you to find what you love to do and what scares you the most. What are your biggest professional fears? Let those motivate you to fuel your success in business and life.

Trust me, you will embarrass yourself. You will motivate others without knowing it. You will do good. You will do bad. You will win the hearts of many, and you will be a failure to others. This unfortunately is the circle of life. Some of your favorite coaches applied for head job after head job, only to get turned down. Some eventually got the job they wanted, only to get fired like Bill Belichick. Denzel Washington wanted to act on Broadway thirty years before making Broadway history in *Fences* in the same building where he was turned down years before. Agent Nicole Lynn was laughed at in the rain when she went to meet with her first recruit. The top player in the NFL Draft years later chose her to represent him without ever meeting her, because he heard that story on YouTube. Steven Trout, Head Baseball Coach, and Texarkana legend, made history with his 2022 Texas State Bobcat team, coaching them to their best year in school history. The year before the team had the worst season in the program's history. Steph Curry went 0-10 from the three-point line on November 4th, 2016. In his very next game, he set the NBA record for the most three-pointers made in an NBA game with 13.

If you coach enough games, play enough games, and audition for enough roles, eventually, you will do great things. I am sure that Steph Curry was nervous, maybe even hesitant, to shoot that next three-pointer after going 0-10. Without knowing him from anyone, I would like to think he is obsessed with being great since he is one of the greatest players ever. Even great players have feelings and nerves. I am assuming that he fears being average enough that it required him to second-guess himself more than ever during the downtime between those two games. The result was he broke records after being backed into a corner.

These are not stories of people we cannot relate to like you normally hear. Coach Trout went to high school with my wife and worked at our baseball camps at the high school I attended from the time I was 14. I can call, text, or go see Coach Trout at any time. His story is a real-life testimony that we all can relate to. Sure, Steph Curry's dad played in the NBA, but he still was a low-level recruit who attended a college that most of us have never heard of. We all know an undersized guy who can shoot the lights out of the gym. None of them are Steph, do not get me wrong. Is that because he was obsessed with being great and they weren't? I cannot answer that, and we will never know, but I believe so. Why wouldn't I?

You can google any person you have a fond respect for and all you will see is failure after failure around their success. The story goes that Thomas Edison had a thousand bad inventions before coming up with the light bulb. He was obsessed with doing something that would change the world, and he did after several missed attempts. It is not just Edison who is now known as someone who could not fail, even though he failed many times. You can read stories about Leonardo de Vinci and how many failed paintings he did before creating the Mona Lisa, or Michelangelo and the Sistine Chapel. Seriously, look up other works by Vincent Van Gogh before and after Starry Night. You can spend your entire life doing mediocre work and be considered a failure. Then one day, in a matter of minutes, you are one of the greatest that ever lived and will be remembered forever.

Starry Night was painted in 1889. I was born in 1989. If that does not blow your mind, I do not know what will. One hundred years later, one piece of artwork lives on, and has made a bigger impact on the world than anything I have done in the last 34 years of being alive. Hopefully, this book will change that.

In my first round of writing, I had these split into two chapters, but I could not help but notice that the message was the same. Unfortunately, we will never know exactly what Edison, da Vinci, van Gogh, or anyone else from that era was obsessed with or scared of. What we do know is that we have timeless work in their professions that will last until the end of time. Moments like that do not happen as a hobby one night at Painting with A Twist while drinking with friends. Countless days, months, and years of failure left a legacy one can only dream of. One hundred years from now their work will be more famous than it is today. If that does not make you want to work hard to leave a legacy, I have no idea what will.

I challenge you to write down what you want to be remembered for. Also, write down what you are obsessed with and scared of. Those three things tell a story. Some people will live a good life, with minimal funds, minimal travel, and minimal friends, and will die in happiness. There is nothing wrong with that. It is not the life I want to have. I want to be remembered for helping people and believing in people. I hope to give one of our players or coaches the battery in their back they need to grow up and continue to change the world the way I dreamed of but with their own personal twist. Teachers, doctors, coaches, law enforcement, and pastors touch and mold more lives than anyone, and do it all for the worst pay and hours worked you can imagine. Ironically, a group of teachers who make at best 50K a year are the ones molding the next young doctor who will come along to cure cancer. One bad teacher teaching their 4th-grade class every day for 30 years that their dreams are too big could set that community back a lifetime. Being a teacher should have strict requirements to apply for, with the best pay and benefits. If the world rewarded the brightest and most gifted humans to be teachers, they could teach a lifetime of knowledge to the next generation. Just like Steve Landers, Jr. did for me.

I realize that doctors make a lot of money, but Doctor Cannon does not make nearly enough money for what he did to save my dad's life during his heart attack. Or the doctor who saved his life during his surgery right after birth. Your profession does not define you. Your fears do not define you. Your obsessions do not define you. What defines you is the legacy you leave behind, the lives you touched, and how you changed the world when you had the opportunity to do so. Alex Wyche, the founder of Minority Baseball Prospects, said it best on a social media post, "The goal isn't to live forever! The goal is to create something that does!"

Walt Disney once asked, "Why do we have to grow up?" Outside of the obvious answers of having adult responsibilities, it does make you think. We talked earlier about the child-like carefree *you can do whatever you want to do in life* attitude that everyone believes in is true, so maybe Walt's question was right. Why do we have to grow up? The imagination inside of each of us keeps us young at heart regardless of age.

This chapter was the easiest to write because it is something I am passionate about. I love helping people and my community. I love telling my story. Not because it is about me, but because I believe my story is relatable. I think deep down we all want to be our own boss, sleep until 11 every day, hire all our family and friends, and leave a legacy that people will remember 100 years from now. It is important to know that to do all those things like I hope to do, you are going to fail a bunch along the way.

# Do Not Allow Self-Doubt to Kill Your Faith

*"The only way to build a masterpiece
is to start with a blank canvas."*
– Jim Collins

I cannot tell you the number of times I dreamed about writing a book. Here we are in Chapter 10, where you are reading about those dreams. One of the themes throughout this book is personal dreams. That is intentional, as I am a glass-half-full guy who wants to be surrounded by positive, reassuring words and mottos. I had to address the importance of your dreams several times before discussing the killer of all dreams: self-doubt.

## Avoiding Self-Doubt

Self-doubt is as dangerous as any drug there is. It will destroy you from the inside before you get started. It has shattered many dreams, visions, and long-term plans. I like to think that self-doubt is roaming, and I can avoid that monster by having more success, but he still gets to me. Self-doubt can arise from a random post with someone saying that you are a terrible person or dragging your name and character through the mud. For a split second, you think, "You know, maybe they are right." Trust me, they are not right.

Faith is what turns dreams into reality. Of course, hard work, waiting your turn, and a bit of luck are also in that equation. Faith is the actual connection that allows the dream to see itself into a reality. This could be faith in yourself, your dreams, or your loved ones, or faith in God for putting you in the position to capitalize.

Most importantly, you must have faith in yourself to achieve your dreams. I have some wild dreams and goals, some of which I'm not sure I deserve to dream about pursuing. My faith in myself allows me to set the bar as high as possible for myself, my family, my team, and my business. It is easy to cut corners to get by, especially when the norm in most professions is to complain about what you don't have. Often, we go long periods without experiencing business or family problems while achieving some personal success, and we take our dreams and faith for granted. We expect things to remain status quo, which is self-doubt's favorite position.

## Faith

Self-doubt loves playing the victim, making it hard to see success as more than luck or a rare moment and achieving personal goals like making *40 Under 40* and *23 People to Watch in '23*. I was thrilled to be named to the *40 People Under 40 to Watch* list. Overconfident, I expected to also be included on the *22 People to Watch in 2022* list, but I wasn't, shaking my confidence and feeding self-doubt. However, in 2023, I was selected as one of five for the *People to Watch in '23* list. The magazine's editor renamed the article "People to Watch in '23" instead of "23 People to Watch in '23."

Life is funny sometimes, and I know it is part of God's plan. I had faith my dreams would come true, making this an extraordinary moment. I went from not being one of the 22 picked the year before to being one of only five chosen for 2023.

## Faith in Your Spouse

Faith extends beyond oneself, especially in a spouse. My wife, Alisha, is a perfect example. She's been instrumental in my life, supporting my career and dreams, strengthening our family with wise decisions, and maintaining our marriage. Her belief in me has empowered me to pursue opportunities I never imagined. Her faith drives me toward my goals. If you are not as lucky as me, and your significant other does not have faith in you, try hitting small goals and milestones to prove you are deserving of having their faith placed in you.

## Faith in Your Employees

Owning a business requires faith in your team to take the company to the next level. Belief in your own standards and policies is also essential. For employees, this faith extends to trusting that their efforts are recognized and will lead to career growth. Trusting others outside your family can be challenging since their true perceptions of you are unknown. People are inherently driven by their desires, like promotions or personal gains, creating a continuous cycle of wants.

I can't coach all 25 Sticks teams each summer or build personal relationships with the parents of each player. I need to have faith in my staff to uphold our company's integrity. Don't fool yourself; challenges are inevitable in any business.

## Faith in Your Customers

Having faith in your customers—or, in my case, players—is crucial to maintaining accountability and ensuring your brand remains reputable. One leading indicator of success is a program's retention rate. Losing players each year requires introspection and change. This holds true for businesses experiencing a drop in loyal customers. Customer faith is vital; they put their faith directly in products they trust and enjoy.

Customer feedback can be direct, such as specific critiques of a product or service. For example, "I do not like this jersey design" or "We want to play a different schedule." Or you may receive feedback indirectly through a third party or by a customer's continued (or discontinued) patronage. Recognize and express thanks to those who support you, especially through tough times, reinforcing their faith in your brand.

## Faith in Your Competition

Faith in competition can be as important as faith within your own business. The Sticks Fall League was a huge success, and when our competitors announced they were having a fall league, I knew we had set the standard. Successfully innovating and setting trends that others follow is a sign that we are ahead in the game.

Our proof of concept opened the door for others to franchise our idea. It would take at least 16 teams to pull off the Fall League franchise concept we envisioned.

Our creative team does a great job creating something organically, only to see regional or local competitors do something similar. When competitors become reflections of your past achievements, it underscores the importance of continuing to innovate and maintain the lead, reaffirming your faith in the competitive process.

A good friend once told me a competing company was building a similar business. They would do the same for anything he would post on his site or order locally. He was annoyed and probably a little nervous. I said, "How great is that for you? If it's true, when times get hard for them, they will have no new ideas or concepts to bring to the table. You will be first to market, first to announce, first to adjust, and first to keep customers. They will never be able to catch up."

It's always good to look at the situation from different angles. The Sticks will never run out of ideas, color schemes, or any other concepts imaginable. I have faith in that. I also have faith that our competition will let me know when we are not putting out the work that we need to put out.

## Faith in a Higher Power

This is the most important paragraph in this book, where I discuss the importance of faith in Jesus Christ. I genuinely believe that without him, none of this is possible. My stories aren't realistic, and it isn't likely to happen again this way. When I think about how we got to this point, it is impossible not to feel that the Lord has put His hand on me directly and wants me to use my story to help change the world.

Alisha grew up in the church. Her dad never missed a moment when the lights were on at church, from Sunday service to a Wednesday choir practice. After her dad passed away, she stepped away from church for a brief time. I didn't grow up attending church regularly. We went occasionally and were baptized, but we didn't go every week. During the COVID lockdown, she explained to me that she was worried that if something happened to me, I would not get into Heaven. We started attending church with her mom, and it was our best decision ever. We have the greatest pastor we could ask for in Brother Tim Montgomery, and a great church in Oasis Church and we are proud to be members.

You can't always explain faith, but you can believe in it. I cannot always explain the Sticks, but I believe in the organization. I also believe God is using me to tell my story to impact many lives through baseball and the Sticks to make that possible. If you are reading this and unsure of your goals or faith, I encourage you to read "In a Pit with a Lion on a Snowy Day" by Mark Batterson. Reading that book changed my life, and I know it will be the best book you have ever read about faith, behind the Bible.

Written words are important to the human race because documented ideas and thoughts can last hundreds of thousands of years. I often wonder how some legacies and stories last longer than others. Ben Franklin, George Washington, Martin Luther King, Jr., William Shakespeare, and the list goes on, were just like you and me. We all possess something special inside of us, and our talent is timeless to mankind. One of the reasons that it is timeless is because we all have written words to read any time we want to. I hope long after I am gone, the words in this book and my story will help change lives and the world.

Don't allow self-doubt to ruin many great things for you. I have seen the most talented players consider not trying out for a team because they doubt their abilities. I have witnessed self-doubt destroy and delay even my own dreams, like writing this book. Do not let self-doubt take your dreams away from you. You owe it to yourself to have faith in something you believe in and make it happen. Self-doubt cannot stop what you refuse to let happen.

I am a dreamer, and I have dreams that you would not believe that I hope to pull off. I must have faith in myself and not let self-doubt kick in, or I will never accomplish my goals. I also must have faith in Alisha that she will believe in me and support my dreams. I must have faith that my employees and business partners believe in my dreams and have faith in me as a leader. I must have faith that the market will like the new dreams I present to them and that they will be a support system to make them work. I must have the ultimate faith that my dreams are aligned with what Jesus's plans are for me and that He will put me in the right places.

## Leaving a Legacy

I know by now you are thinking, "How can I change the world or leave an impact in my business like that Sticks have in the baseball world?" Only you can answer that question. Every person's answer will be different and will be a piece of a much bigger puzzle that can help save the world over time.

Steve Jobs created the iPhone. He did not know that future iPhone models would include features to help change the world. We now know things like police brutality do exist because bystanders have recorded them in the act. We can hold on to the precious keepsake photos and videos that mean so much to us, like our children's first steps using our iPhone's camera. We can work from anywhere in the world because we have access to everything we need in the palm of our hands.

Steve Jobs did not do all these things by himself. He used his vision and passion to create something for many people to use. Maybe someone reading this will create an app to push the world forward or use social media for good. The ideas and hope are endless, but it is important to know you do not have to do it all alone. Something you are passionate about will play a small piece in the bigger picture, and eventually, it will all make sense. I had no idea when we started our first team that we would get to impact the lives of 400-plus players each year, impacting generations for years to come.

# Epilogue

*"It's only scary because you have never done it"*
– Jesse Cole

In the final chapter, written from a beach in San Diego near our Airbnb, I reflect on the extraordinary experiences of my career and this week. Earlier, I discussed the power of vision boards for achieving seemingly unattainable dreams and goals. Currently, I'm living what once felt like an unachievable dream.

Coaching at the Area Code event has been a dream of mine for a long time. It's the summer's most prominent individual event, featuring top players from the United States and Canada. The event is a gathering of elite talent represented by eight MLB teams: the White Sox, Reds, Yankees, Royals, Brewers, Rangers, Nationals, and A's. Each team is coached by professional scouts, drawing an audience of pro scouts, agents, and college coaches. It's an extraordinary opportunity for these players.

My involvement with the 2023 White Sox Team began through discussions with Rob Cummings about our Sticks players and potential recruits from the Midwest for the White Sox. As these talks progressed, Tim Decker negotiated with Area Code for Decker Sports to sponsor the event. Once it became known that I would attend with Decker Sports and had connections with some of the future White Sox Area Code players, Rob and JJ Lalley invited me to join their coaching staff. Mike Shirley signed off on my coaching role, making it official. I am deeply thankful to these three.

At this point in my career, I seldom feel nervous, but arriving at our first meeting for the event, I felt out of place and nervous, which was likely apparent to others. As one of the few non-scout or non-professional attendees, I was apprehensive until I encountered familiar faces like JD French from the Atlanta Braves and Matt Ransom from the New York Yankees. Their presence, due to past collaborations, eased my anxiety and made me feel better about the situation.

As the players arrived, I recognized many familiar faces. Five out of our 30-man roster were former or current players with the Sticks, and several others had competed against us. Among them were talented Razorback commit Lance Davis, Arizona State University commit Lawson Ward, and infielder Drew Dickerson, an Oklahoma commit and a remarkable individual who had a successful summer with the Sticks. Ole Miss commit Slade Caldwell and LSU infield commit Kale Fountain, both past Sticks players, were also there. Gradually, my nervousness subsided.

However, identifying coaches among the crowd was challenging because everyone was wearing their respective MLB team gear. For instance, a coach from the Houston Astros could be part of the White Sox Team's coaching staff, wearing Astros gear instead of the White Sox. This added to the confusion as nearly sixty people gathered for the first time.

Mike Shirley briefly addressed everyone first. It was immediately obvious that he was in charge. Following him, JJ outlined three simple rules for the players: 1) be on time, 2) play hard, and 3) have fun. He then asked each coach to introduce themselves, including their name, origin, and affiliated program. As the introductions continued, I felt increasingly modest about my role, especially when I realized there were 18 coaches, including myself. I could not help but think that I had probably wasted my time coming.

Among the coaches were Dan Budreika from the White Sox, and Justin Munson of the Philadelphia Phillies, known for his legendary junior college coaching. Others included Steve Abney from the A's and Scott Melvin of the Kansas City Royals, Andy Stack from the Reds, who all mentored the players throughout the weekend.

Eric Wordekemper of the Miami Marlins excelled in guiding the pitchers. Ty Nichols from the Chicago Cubs impressed me with his character, as did Brett Baldwin with the Rockies, James Goodwin of the Washington Nationals, Joe Bisenius from the Minnesota Twins, David Peterson with the Los Angeles Dodgers, and Todd Shafer from the San Francisco Giants. Being part of this remarkable group of coaches was a privilege.

My self-doubt was obvious as I stood alongside 17 highly respected coaches and professional scouts. However, this feeling dissipated as practice began and players impressively hit home runs during batting practice. Anticipating a challenging first game against the historically talented Texas Rangers, I was preparing mentally when Andy Stack and David Pearson approached me with an unexpected request: to coach first base. This left me momentarily speechless, as it had been nearly eight years since I last held that position, reigniting my insecurities. I had little time to dwell on these thoughts because we were the visiting team and I needed to head to first base. Two pitches later, Slade Caldwell was on base, and we were off and ready to go.

The most challenging aspect of coaching first base was managing the players' equipment while they were on base. This included a variety of gear: elbow guards, arm guards, leg guards, thumb protectors, oven mitts, and batting gloves. During innings with multiple base runners, I found myself having to store all their gear in the opposing team's bullpen until the final out of the inning.

Offensively, we were by far the best team there, making my role as a base coach particularly enjoyable. A veteran scout remarked to Rob that this was the most impressive offensive team he had ever seen at the event. We navigated pool play with ease, thanks to the players' consistent performance against tough pitchers. Facing speeds of 94-96 mph, we consistently scored high, defeating teams like the Texas Rangers (11-2), Northwest Yankees (11-1), Southeast Reds (13-0), and Northwest Royals (7-4).

Key players like Caleb Bonemar (Virginia), Cole Crafton (Alabama), Sir Jamison Jones (Illinois State), Tyson Lewis (Arkansas), and Garrett Shull (Oklahoma State), along with the previously mentioned Sticks players, made the opposing pitchers work hard. This team was truly special, and their talent and camaraderie made coaching and spending the week with them an unforgettable experience.

In the first-ever outright Area Code Championship Game, we faced the Yankees again in a rematch. Despite having scored 42 runs in four games against some of the best amateur pitchers in the United States, we were limited to two runs in the championship, ultimately losing 10-2. Baseball can be unforgiving at times.

I often remind players that being a champion doesn't necessarily require winning a trophy, celebrating with a dog pile, or triumphing in the last game of a tournament. This was the essence of my message to the team post-game. These highly talented players were remarkable individuals who were easy to interact with in the dugout or off the field. The most disappointing aspect of losing the Championship Game was the conclusion of the event itself; I believe everyone would have liked to have spent another day with this group.

Fortunately, our coaching staff never witnessed any negative behavior from our players, as we decisively won most games until the final day. I'd like to think our players would have maintained their composure and professionalism even if we had faced losses earlier in the tournament. The absence of three key players in the Championship Game, due to their commitments to the Baseball Factory All-American Game scheduled to start the next day, was a setback. With the constant occurrence of "can't miss" events, I'm still contemplating whether this is ultimately beneficial or detrimental.

The inclusion of this chapter in my book is a testament that anything is possible. As a high school manager with limited professional baseball experience, beyond being an associate scout for the Dodgers, my involvement with the Chicago White Sox at the Area Code event as a first base coach is extraordinary. The team I was lucky enough to coach on is considered by some as the best in the event's history. How awesome is that? Acknowledging this achievement motivates me to pursue even more ambitious goals, those so far-fetched that they might invite skepticism or disbelief, even from my supporters. I am not sure if people who believed in me saw this coming, because I know I didn't.

This unexpected journey has inspired me to revise my vision board and my list of goals, adding some that are so audacious they even give me pause. But the next step is clear: to turn these seemingly improbable dreams into reality.

# Reflection

*"If you would not be forgotten as soon as you are dead and rotten, either write things worth reading or do things worth the writing"*
– Ben Franklin

So many once-in-a-lifetime wow moments have happened that I am starting to take them for granted. Regularly, there seems to be another event I'm invited to or an article written about me that makes me have to pinch myself. I planned to write about each of these moments for personal reflection and motivation for readers, but it was challenging to fit them into the previous chapters. Writing this chapter felt therapeutic, allowing me to relive significant life moments granted by baseball, though it initially seemed vain. I am grateful to those who have let me be a part of their lives and share in these remarkable experiences. The theme of this entire book has been a very unlikely one from the moment we started Sticks Baseball. Truthfully, my entire career has been like that. I am so thankful that baseball has blessed me with so many experiences.

\* \* \* \* \*

I want to convey my joy and excitement for the future of Sticks Baseball, and how our 2024 summer is shaping up. On paper, our 2025 group appears to be the best team we've ever had for our Sticks Baseball 17U Brewster/White Sox Scout Team.

Landon Schaefer, an Arkansas commit and Team USA infielder, returns as our captain. He excelled last summer, playing up an age group as our shortstop and batting second. Landon's versatility extends to the outfield as well. Also rejoining us is infielder Jackson Akin, who similarly played up last summer. We'll rely on him as our key hitter in the cleanup spot and third baseman next summer.

Our pitching staff is one of the best in the country, and on pace to keep up with the tradition of strong arms leading the way. Returning players include Razorback commits Grant Wren and Mark Brissey, Tennessee commit Tyler Wood, and Florida commit Minjae Seo, all of whom played up an age group last summer. Joining them are standout pitchers from our 16U team, including Razorback commits McLane Moody, Russ Martin, and Jaison Delamar, as well as Louisiana Tech University commit Caleb Short and Wichita State commit right hander Grant Karnes. Additionally, we have two of the top uncommitted talents in Texas: right-hander Luke Flanagan and left-hander Kael Cole. All these pitchers are coming off impressive summers with Sticks 16U Slayton.

We've strengthened our team with new additions, including Kansas State committed twins Max and Sam Bettis from Kansas, and Xavier commit Dillon Askew. Our roster also features several other two-way returners like University of Louisiana –Monroe standout Jarret Halter, who has been all-state in both the field and on the mound, and Razorback commit Walt Jones, who hit lead off for 16U group the summer prior. From Connecticut, we welcome Princeton commit Bennett Crerar, an infielder/ outfielder and an Area Code participant for the New York Yankees team. Known for both his exceptional character and skill, Bennett is slated to bat third at the start of the summer. Another out-of-state recruit, Cal commit Nikko Taylor from

El Sobrante, joins our infield following his Area Code team participation. Additionally, we're excited to welcome former Razorback standout Blake Baxendale to our coaching staff.

Not only are 17Us looking extremely special for the summer of 2024, but our entire program top to bottom is in a beautiful place. Our 2026 is among our best in recent years, led by Razorback commits Spencer Browning, Hunter Rose, and Marcus Bates, and Memphis commit Parker King. Recent NCAA rule changes have affected the commitment process, leaving highly talented players like Owen Roach, Ethan Carswell, Owen Davenport, and Buck Anderson, among others, with a prime opportunity to make a significant impact this summer.

Our freshman class, though not as deep as other years, includes highly talented players. Among them is Ty Holt, younger brother of University of Arkansas star and Sticks alumnus Peyton Holt. Ty stands out as a star catcher. Jaxson Adcock, a shortstop, leads the group and ranks among the Midwest's best players, continuing our tradition of exceptional shortstops. His future, along with that of other promising players like Jackson Teutsch, Jacob Maynard and Gage Klober from Arkansas, and Eli Field from Florida, is exceptionally bright.

\* \* \* \* \*

When we started Sticks Baseball, we dreamed about having a Perfect Game All-American. Witnessing Braylon Bishop play in the 2020 Perfect Game All-American Game in Oklahoma City was a pivotal moment for Sticks Baseball. It was unforgettable to see the result of his hard work and to share this moment with his family, particularly his father Nick Bishop. The sense of pride in having a Sticks player in that game is still exhilarating.

Two years before, Alisha and I traveled to Chicago to watch Jaden Hill pitch at Wrigley Field, home of the Chicago Cubs, in the Under Armour All-American Game. Jaden had worked hard to transform himself into a top prospect and left that event recognized by Baseball America as having the "best change-up in amateur baseball." The joy and pride of his parents, Kenneith and Nikki, and his siblings Kentrell and Aleya, as well as the entire community, were proud. To see that in real-time is among the top moments that will last forever.

\* \* \* \* \*

Attending the Rawlings Gold Glove Dinner at The Plaza in New York is an unforgettable experience, one I've had the privilege of experiencing multiple times. I am deeply grateful to Steve Napolitano and Steve Cohen for their generosity in ensuring my family's attendance at this premier baseball event. In 2022, bringing Kyle Slayton as my guest was particularly meaningful, knowing how much he wanted to attend. Looking back and seeing pictures of Kyle and me with Nolan Arenado, Andruw Jones, Jeremy Pena, Doc Gooden, and Brendan Donovan, among others, underscore the value of unexpected opportunities and the remarkable gatherings we are sometimes invited to.

\* \* \* \* \*

Andrew Guerra, an agent with Roc Nation, has become a close friend, even attending our wedding. His role comes with benefits, and he has always treated Alisha and me exceptionally well. Knowing CC Sabathia is one of my favorite players, Andrew ensured we were on the field for Sabathia's final career game. Although I had met CC several times, witnessing his last game was important to me. This opportunity also led to meeting Aaron Judge, another once-in-a-lifetime experience.

One of my most cherished career memories involves an event I was unable to attend. Andrew and Roc Nation invited Alisha and me to Marcus Stroman's Shugo product release party at the 40/40 Club in New York City, an event with an exclusive guest list. Unfortunately, our luggage was delayed on the day we flew in, we had nothing to wear and missed the event. Just knowing that someone would want me to attend an event like that at the 40/40 Club is one of my top wow moments.

\* \* \* \* \*

Being named to the "Most Influential People in Travel Baseball" list by JKR and John Sparaco is an unforgettable honor. It's remarkable to be included among just six industry leaders, alongside Evin Einhardt, Nelly Gonzalez, Marc Nellist, Jeffy Petty, and Ajay Vulimiri. Being recognized with these legends of our sport is a privilege I hold close to my heart.

\* \* \* \* \*

Another significant accolade is PBR and Lakepoint Sports naming our victory over Nelson Baseball in the PBR Showdown Championship as the "2022 Game of the Year." Considering the thousands of games played at Lakepoint each year, this recognition as the Game of the Year is an extraordinary honor. A key moment in this game was Jayce Blaylock's opportunity to hit with runners in scoring position during extra innings to win the game for the good guys.

\* \* \* \* \*

Our 2023 run in Jupiter is an emotional highlight for me. The coaching staff, players, and parents formed an exceptional group, the kind you wish to be around every day. Our triumph in winning our pool, and the players' outstanding performance, filled me with pride.

In the playoffs, we faced the Phillies Scout Team, securing a 1-0 victory with a walk-off in the bottom of the 7th inning, advancing us to the final 16. However, our next game against Trosky proved challenging. Trailing 4-1 in the 7th inning, we rallied to tie the game at 4-4. A subsequent 2-hour rain delay and a change of fields unfortunately disrupted our momentum. We traded runs in the 8th and 9th innings but ultimately lost to a walk-off. I know that everyone in our dugout would have loved to see what would have happened without the delay, but that's why you play the game.

\* \* \* \* \*

We carried over our success from the end of 2023 into 2024 on a good note. In January, we opened at the Perfect Game MLK Tournament in Phoenix, AZ. Since our first participation in 2018, we consistently reached the Final Four of this event, winning it twice. Our team featured a core group of franchise players, including Drew Dickerson, Conner Cunningham, Brenton Clark, Lawson Ward, and Schaefer. To enhance our roster, we added several talented players.

Among the newcomers was Slade Caldwell, a top 20 player in his class who is universally projected as a first-round MLB Draft pick. He led off in every game and covered center field. Another notable addition was Grady Emerson, a TCU commit who played at shortstop and second base. As the top-ranked player in the country for 2026, Emerson, at just 15, won the MVP of the 18U event. Despite our strong performance, finishing the tournament with a 5-1 record, we were defeated in the Championship by Baum Bat in both the 18U and 17U age divisions.

\* \* \* \* \*

Attempting to put on paper all the remarkable moments Alisha and I have shared in the past fifteen years is an overwhelming task. Waiting nearly a decade to propose underscores the need for a memorable approach. Proposing to Alisha in Central Park in New York City still takes the cake as my most nerve-wracking experience and one of our greatest wow moments. This iconic moment was made possible by our involvement with the Sticks and the opportunities provided by baseball.

A last-minute trip the week of the event almost ruined the proposal. Steve Landers helped me get the engagement ring through his jeweler, despite the limited time and without me seeing the ring beforehand. I picked it up and we jumped on the plane the same day. I booked a photographer on Craigslist at 11:45 pm the night before we did it. As the saying goes, "All's well that ends well."

\* \* \* \* \*

I could talk endlessly about personal experiences that might seem inconsequential to others, but reflecting on these surreal moments while writing this has been a profound experience for me. I am immensely grateful for the extraordinary life God has blessed me with, far beyond my wildest dreams. The aim of this chapter is not to brag about various events but to inspire you to recognize your potential and the limitless achievements within your grasp.

Reflecting on what's next is a recurring theme as I write this chapter. Numerous projects are in development, which I'm eager to share, but they have yet to materialize. As much as I don't want to jinx anything, I feel like I would be doing this story a disservice if I did not mention them when it comes to wow moments in my life.

I'm especially honored to be named the 2024 Ambassador of Baseball Award recipient by Victor Feld and the Greater New York Athletic Alliance. In November 2024, I'll have the privilege of delivering a speech at Russo's on the Bay in Long Island, New York, during their annual black-tie event—an opportunity I cherish deeply.

\* \* \* \* \*

This comes at the perfect time, as I've never given a public speech beyond addressing our players. I'm honored to have been invited by Ryan Brownlee to speak at the 2026 ABCA National Clinic. This prestigious event represents the pinnacle of baseball coaching clinics and has been a long-standing goal of mine. Witnessing Jeff Petty and Nate Trosky speak at the 2023 clinic in Nashville, TN, and their representation of travel baseball in a forum dominated by high school, college, and professional coaches, inspired me to confront my fear of public speaking and contribute as well.

While discussing these future plans might seem premature, both events are currently scheduled, and I am really excited about them. As this book approaches its final stages of writing and editing, discussions with various publishing companies and writing agents have highlighted the likelihood of public speaking engagements that accompany a successful publication. Hopefully, this preparation is a step toward sharing our story on a larger platform.

* * * * *

As this project concludes, I urge you to consider your future and the 'wow' moments you anticipate. These moments often arise not spontaneously but are byproducts of your dreams and visions. Reflect on 'wow' moments that involve others and the fulfillment that comes from being part of their achievements. It could be a child preparing for college, a sibling or friend on the verge of a career milestone, and your role in these events.

Consider long-term planning beyond your immediate goals. For instance, Alisha and I eagerly await our niece's transition from middle to high school. I'm already strategizing how I can build a business for her to manage after her college graduation in 2033.

How can I do something this week to help my brother's children be successful when the time comes? Lucky for me, they are not born yet, so I have more time on them. My point is I challenge you to start long-term planning and create something inclusive, fostering an environment where we can impact as many lives as possible.

# Acknowledgments

It would be difficult to list everyone who has made this project possible. Over the last 34 years, many mentors and helping hands have helped mold me into who I am today. There is no story to tell without you guys pouring into me when you did not have to.

Without Jesus Christ, none of this is possible. I have no idea why he reached down and put his hand on me when he did, but I am forever grateful for the unconditional love he has for me.

My father, Dave Brewster, supported me when others told him that I needed to get a "real" job. He gave my brother and me the keys and resources to be successful when he did not have to. He would work everyday rain or sunshine, sick or healthy, to ensure we did not go without. I am forever indebted to you. I love you!

To Sandy Brewster, thank you so much for coming into our family and making sure that my dad was happy. I love you!

To my beautiful wife, Alisha, who has told me on more than one occasion that she is not reading this book because she has lived through it. Marrying you was the best decision I ever made. I hope everyone is lucky enough to find love with their significant other like I have with you. I look forward to creating more memories together. Thank you for staying by my side at all times. I love you!

To my brother, Dylan Brewster, without you, I wouldn't have anyone to keep me grounded and humble. It has been just as fun to watch you grow into your own stardom. I look forward to doing great things together in the future. I love you!

To Alisha's side of the family who has taken me in as one of your own, I am forever indebted to Lisa, Alex, Jordan, Eden, Scott, Christa, Loryn, Camryn, Eric, Alicia, Isaiah, Erica, and most importantly Darlene Morales. I love you all!

To the man who taught me everything I know in business, and half what I know in baseball. I am forever in debt to Steve Landers, Jr., and his family. I thank God every day that you decided to start the Sticks. Not only you Coach, but Karmen, Tripp, Aubree, and Annika, I love you guys!

Speaking of the Sticks, none of this happens without the constant support and impact from guys like Evan Hamm, Johnny Tollett, Zac Bottoms, Jason Kelly, Kyle Slayton, Brett Huskey, Tanner Rockwell, Blaine Tanner, Tommy Richardson, Jacob Richardson, Cesar Abreu, Dyllon Brownmiller, Shane Halter, Frank Halter, Jeff Sullivan, Kevin Browning, Rocky King, Cory Lambert, Cason Tollett, Nick Bishop, Andrew Dion, Connor Anderson, Jeremy Myers, Willie Prince, Karl Carswell, Zach Muldon, Will Hankins, Justin Cunningham, Rafael Thomas, Stephen Barnes, and so many others over the years. Some people have come and gone, and others are just starting to show up every day to help take us to the next level. To each one of you, I truly love you guys.

There is no Sticks or Sticks story to tell without Tyler Sawyer and Dirk Kinney. You two deserve your own paragraph. I have no idea when our run together will be over, but it has been one of the greatest runs in Arkansas baseball history. I love you guys.

To my best friend, Kameron Forte, I owe you so much. You have been there through all the highs and lows, including many moments I can't put in print. You handed me the ring to slide on Alisha's finger at our wedding; it does not get more special than that. I won't mention that you dropped the ring box while doing so. Here is to making more memories together. I love you all, Shallon, Cali, Keaton, Piper, Ike, and Glenda!

There are many other people who I love so much who helped mold me into who I am today. I cannot thank you enough for the friendships you guys have given me. Jared Washington, Jaden Hill, Michael Milum, Shaun Manning, Kyle Davis, Blake Baxendale, Morgan Smith, and so many more, I love you all!

Thank you to everyone at Decker Sports, especially Tim Decker for believing in me and being a mentor to me. Our short time together has been timeless, and I look forward to our future together. Jack Hansen, Josh Pollack, Derek Hemingway, Greg Freivogel, and everyone else in Omaha, I love all of you guys!

Thank you to Coach Will Bolt for giving me a chance, and to Coach Justin Seely for teaching me about communication and recruiting. Our time at Texarkana College was amazing, and I don't think anyone saw this coming for all of us. What a special group it was. Lance Harvell, Travis Wendte, and Brad Flanders, I love all of you guys!

Coach Glenn Welch, Coach Scott Mennie, Coach John McClure, and Texas High as a whole, none of this happens without you guys. I have no idea why you let me hang out in the dugout and tag along on road trips, but it changed my life. I hope I can repay you guys someday. I love all of you guys!

ACKNOWLEDGMENTS

Coach Barry Norton, you were a mentor and a role model before I knew what those were. People can say whatever they want about you, but you have been the greatest gift to my career, and I owe you so much. I love you, Coach!

Jonathan Gosdin, Kevin Huff, TJ Cox, Debbie Huff, and everyone at Genoa Central, I am extremely indebted to you guys. I do not think any of us had any idea of the amount of fun or the history we were making while it was happening. So many Championships and wins but the memories we made off the field still stand out to me. I love you guys!

To Jack Mize and everyone at Main Street Authority, thank you for taking on this project and turning it into a final masterpiece. I will love you guys forever.

Cooper and Drake, you make our lives an adventure and I know how proud of this project you both are. I love you!

It would be impossible to name everyone, unfortunately— although I wish I could. None more than our favorite QB1, we miss you One Five. We love you, Ryan Mallett.

Keep showing up until they give you
all those accolades you feel you deserve.
Until they call you chairman.
Until they call you a genius.
Until they call you the greatest of all time."
~ Jay-Z